P9-CCP-921

ALSO BY EDWARD BALL

Peninsula of Lies

Slaves in the Family

The Sweet Hell Inside

The Genetic Strand

Exploring a Family History Through DNA

Edward Ball

Simon & Schuster
NEW YORK · LONDON · TORONTO · SYDNEY

SIMON & SCHUSTER
Rockefeller Center
1230 Avenue of the Americas
New York, NY 10020

First Simon & Schuster hardcover edition November 2007

Text designed by Paul Dippolito

Manufactured in the United States of America

10 9 8 7 6 5 4 3 2 1

Library of Congress Cataloging-in-Publication Data

Ball, Edward, 1959–
The genetic strand : exploring a family history through DNA / Edward Ball.
p. cm.
Includes index.
1. Ball family. 2. Charleston Region (S.C.)—Biography. 3. Mitochondrial DNA—Analysis. 4. DNA—Analysis. 5. DNA fingerprinting. I. Title.
F279.C453.B35 2007
929'.20973—dc22

2007011513

ISBN-13: 978-0-7432-6658-1
ISBN-10: 0-7432-6658-7

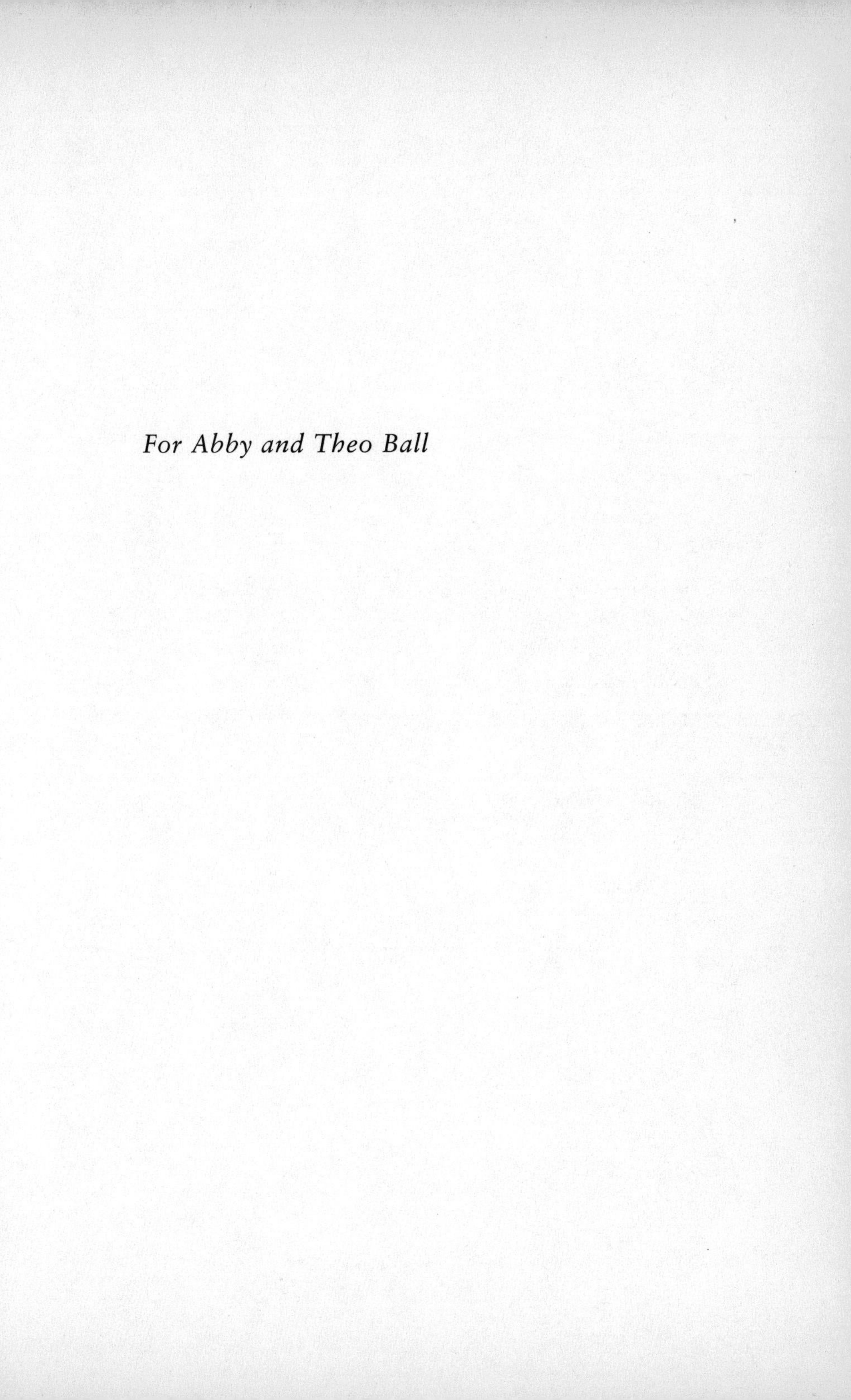

For Abby and Theo Ball

Contents

Before the golden tresses of the dead,
The right of sepulchres, were shorn away,
To live a second life on second head;
Ere beauty's dead fleece made another gay . . .

SHAKESPEARE, SONNET 68

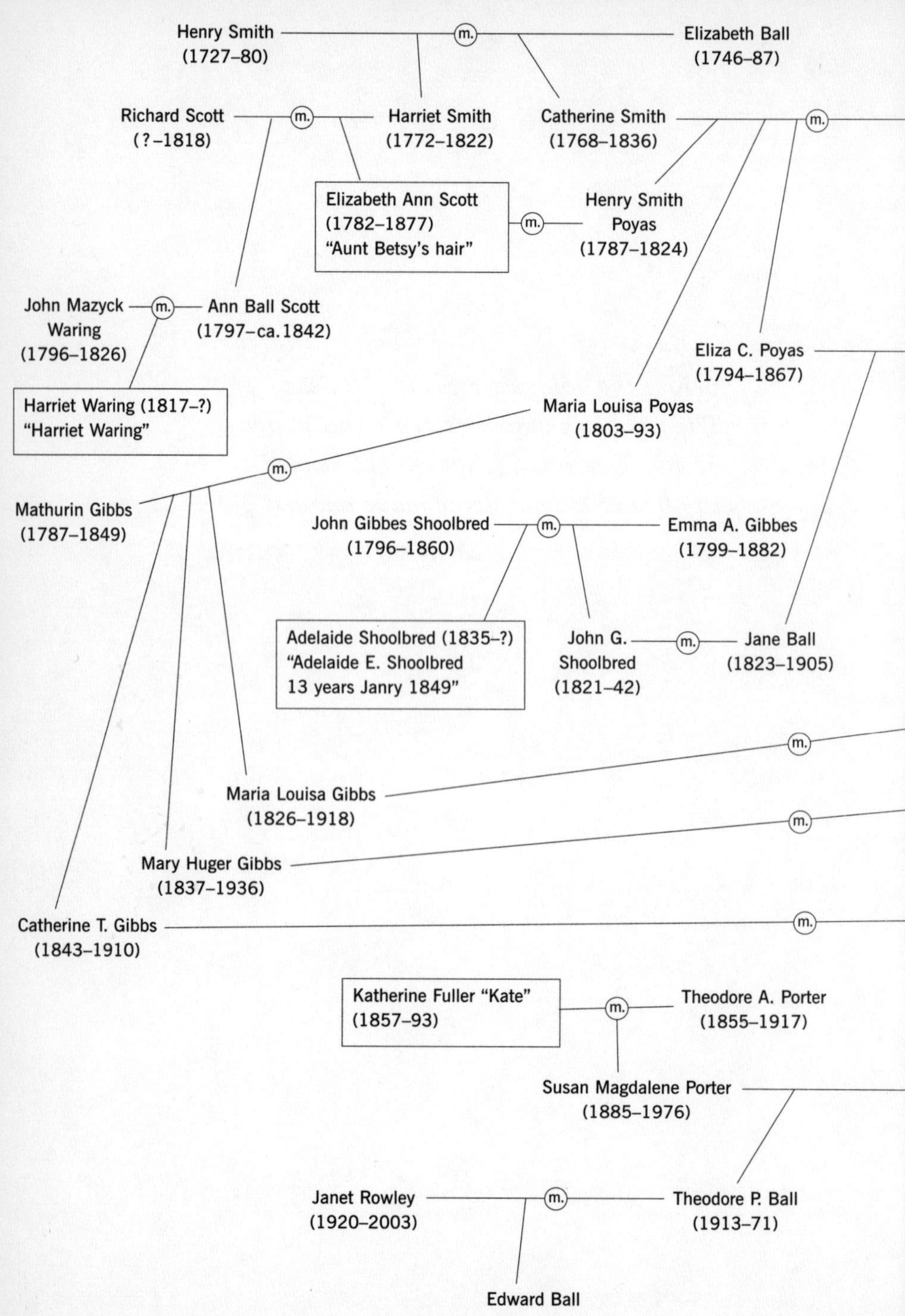

Henry Smith (1727–80)
m.
Elizabeth Ball (1746–87)
Richard Scott (?–1818)
m.
Harriet Smith (1772–1822)
Catherine Smith (1768–1836)
m.
Elizabeth Ann Scott (1782–1877) "Aunt Betsy's hair"
m.
Henry Smith Poyas (1787–1824)
John Mazyck Waring (1796–1826)
m.
Ann Ball Scott (1797–ca.1842)
Eliza C. Poyas (1794–1867)
Harriet Waring (1817–?) "Harriet Waring"
Maria Louisa Poyas (1803–93)
m.
Mathurin Gibbs (1787–1849)
John Gibbes Shoolbred (1796–1860)
m.
Emma A. Gibbes (1799–1882)
Adelaide Shoolbred (1835–?) "Adelaide E. Shoolbred 13 years Janry 1849"
John G. Shoolbred (1821–42)
m.
Jane Ball (1823–1905)
m.
Maria Louisa Gibbs (1826–1918)
m.
Mary Huger Gibbs (1837–1936)
Catherine T. Gibbs (1843–1910)
m.
Katherine Fuller "Kate" (1857–93)
m.
Theodore A. Porter (1855–1917)
Susan Magdalene Porter (1885–1976)
Janet Rowley (1920–2003)
m.
Theodore P. Ball (1913–71)
Edward Ball

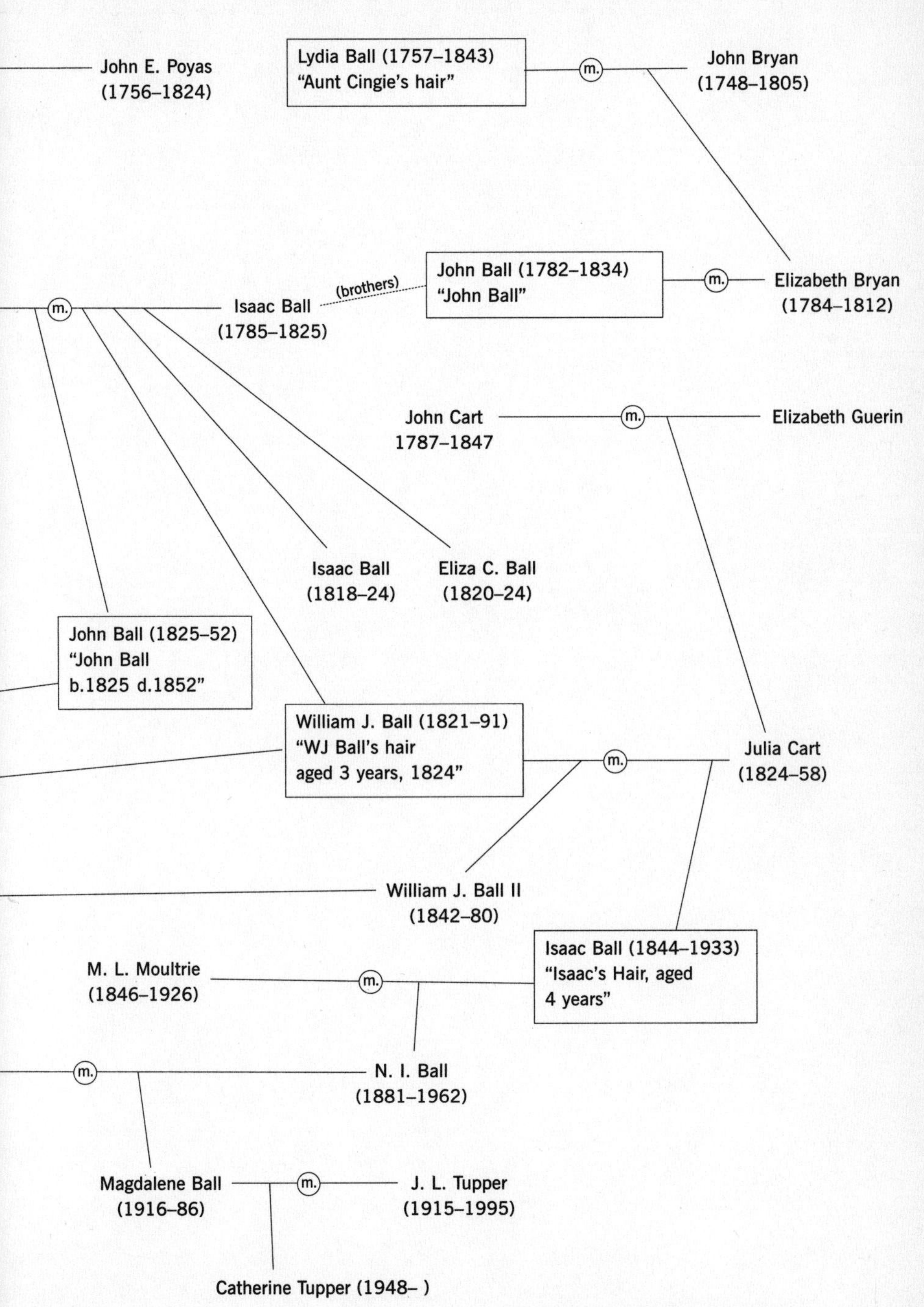
John E. Poyas
(1756–1824)
Lydia Ball (1757–1843)
"Aunt Cingie's hair"
m.
John Bryan
(1748–1805)
m.
Isaac Ball
(1785–1825)
(brothers)
John Ball (1782–1834)
"John Ball"
m.
Elizabeth Bryan
(1784–1812)
John Cart
1787–1847
m.
Elizabeth Guerin
Isaac Ball
(1818–24)
Eliza C. Ball
(1820–24)
John Ball (1825–52)
"John Ball
b.1825 d.1852"
William J. Ball (1821–91)
"WJ Ball's hair
aged 3 years, 1824"
m.
Julia Cart
(1824–58)
William J. Ball II
(1842–80)
Isaac Ball (1844–1933)
"Isaac's Hair, aged
4 years"
M. L. Moultrie
(1846–1926)
m.
m.
N. I. Ball
(1881–1962)
Magdalene Ball
(1916–86)
m.
J. L. Tupper
(1915–1995)
Catherine Tupper (1948–)

The Genetic Strand

Preface

A STRANGE DISCOVERY caused me to write these pages, like the frozen hunters that have fallen out of melting glaciers in the Alps, and thousand-year-old bog people who have surfaced from moors in Ireland. I found something similar to these things, though not an ice-covered mummy. Due to the chance appearance of a stash of ancient DNA, which turned up in the living room, I became, for a couple of years, an amateur forensic examiner. I recommend the experience, except for this part of it: after falling under the scrutiny of genetics, I could no longer be sure who or what I was. Whereas there used to be no doubt.

What follows is a personal investigation of DNA science. It begins with an intimate finding. Many years ago, some distant relatives collected biological material—from themselves. They wanted to preserve it, but they probably didn't expect that someone in the future would want to subject it to laboratory analysis, extract genetic material from it, and draw conclusions about them from the results. Which is what occurred, the events that take place in this book.

After discovering a hoard of family genes, I brought it to the attention of DNA scientists and forensic examiners. I educated myself about molecular biology and the things people do with deoxyribonucleic acid in forensic inquiries and in genetics labs. At the start, possibly the most trenchant thing I knew about DNA, the majestic manual of life, was that up close it looked like the Guggenheim Museum. In part, this was because I'm that suspect thing in the eyes of the scientific enterprise: a nonscientist. Chemistry and biology had never aroused me, and I didn't feel the excitement for the "miracles of science" that the public is called on to admire. Nevertheless, my living room was to become a molecular biology salon, part genetics classroom and part forensics office. I wanted to be entertained and enlightened. I didn't plan on a crisis of identity.

DNA science calls a lot of narcissism into the room. What genes do you carry? Who are you? Where did you come from? People with restless minds go over these things in a loop. The wondering about biological inheritance, what has come from your parents, and, for parents, what's going from you to your children, leaves you vulnerable to half-made answers. But, having returned from a kind of genetic quest, I testify that fantastic discoveries lie along the way, provided you don't think of them as having the truth of religion.

The forensic investigation I planned and the one I got turned out to be very different. Using my unusual collection of DNA, I'd expected to write a genetic profile of a family. By reputation, genetics was that miracle tool that could see through the body, and so I thought it might be possible to document one family's biological nature. It didn't happen. Instead, I've written a story that tracks some of the limits of genetics, rather than showing off its reach. But this result is more interesting, and more disturbing.

My tale has two plots. In the first, it is a scientific travelogue, one person's journey through the field of genes. I visit researchers in their laboratories and habitats, talking to people who do DNA analysis, learning how they do it. In a parallel plot, this book is a piece of family history, though it's a special kind, one made possible by forensics and not solely by memory or research. These pages tell the stories of several people, long dead, whose lives are lighted up by trace biological evidence they left behind. The idea of a genetic family portrait survives, but it's more modest; the surprises come from what the scientists do to the evidence, not from their revelations about it.

When I finished, I realized that I had set up a kind of forensics of the self. An esoteric field that will be of little use to the police, but gratifying to the person who wonders who they "are." It's an old enigma—who you and your family are, your race, your identity—that genetics and detective work promise to decipher in a different way.

The investigation began, dumbly enough, with a mute piece of furniture.

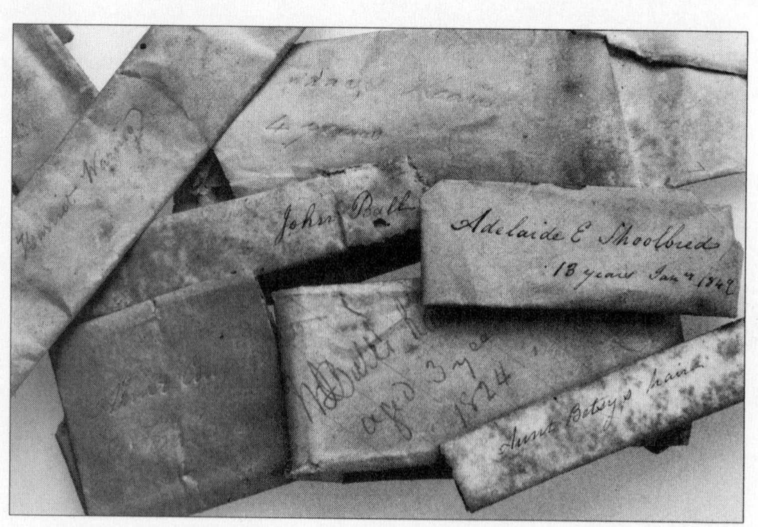
John Bull
Adelaide E Shoolbred
Aunt Betsy's hair

1 *The Desk*

SEVERAL YEARS AGO, I made a disturbing find. It happened when a furniture truck delivered some old things to my house. The truck pulled up, and the men put the things on the sidewalk: one table, six chairs, a four-poster bed, a buffet, and the two halves of an old desk. All were antiques, as well as heirlooms. These relics hadn't come in the usual way, which is, I think, when one acquires, by dignified inheritance, sumptuous rarities belonging to one's family. A cousin had bequeathed this furniture to her brother. He didn't want it, and I had desired it; so I'd paid the new owner a good deal of money to give the things to me. Now, in the afternoon light—not the dim bulbs of storage—this appeared to have been a dubious transaction, because disinterested eyes could see that the things were in bad shape. The most decrepit was the desk, a grand piece of broken bulk and stuck drawers, black from caked wax and dirt. But, compensating for its condition, inside the desk was a strange treasure.

I'd first seen the desk at the aforementioned cousin's house in the suburbs, and she'd talked about its life, how her great-grandmother had owned it, and how her mother had passed it on to her. It had been in family hands since 1800 or so, she said. The desk had a past, something like a story, which may be why people like antiques, because in my experience they don't work as real furniture.

An antiques dealer would call it a secretary and bookcase. Cabinetmakers used to build hundreds of them, but their design is useless to moderns. It had typical construction: two sections that stack on top of each other to make a whole about seven feet tall and four feet wide, refrigerator-scale. The bottom consisted of a three-drawer chest with a flip-down writing surface, while the top, from the waist up, had bookshelves behind cabinet doors. The mammoth leaned to the left because one of its stubby legs had broken off. I put some books under that corner to stand it right.

It was obvious the desk was unusable. To sit at the high writing surface required a stool, and I found it awkward to sit up in the air like Bartleby the scrivener. The wood was scarred like a salad counter, and the interior shelving so delicate and dilapidated that if one touched a letter slot, it might crumble. On the other hand, the desk was quite beautiful beneath its raggedness, and it smelled musty, like sheep. The smell and appearance gave it buried layers of meaning.

The thing needed cleaning, the frozen drawers had to be unstuck, and the crevices wiped of grit. And with that, the wobbly desktop dropped open, revealing six cubbyholes for letters. In the midst of the letter slots was a small door, about seven inches square. The place for liquor? A money safe?

The door had a lock with a tiny skeleton key, which still worked, and behind the door was a little cabinet space, with a bit of scalloped molding for decoration. With a touch, this molding moved, then it moved farther and came out: it was the face of a little drawer, though it had no knob. The drawer would have been invisible except to one who knew it was there, which I did not. It opened easily, and from a puff of dust it was clear it hadn't been disturbed in a long time. A hiding place. Later, I learned that other secretaries of the same period often possessed similar hidden drawers, stealth compartments used by their owners for whatever secret purpose.

Inside the little drawer, there appeared to be a number of tiny envelopes, each the size of a matchbook. On closer inspection, the envelopes turned out to be folded pieces of paper, with a name and hand-scribbled dates written on each. Their blotchy yellow color and the formal handwriting suggested the folded bits had been stored a hundred or more years ago. Most of the names were familiar. They were people from my father's family, all of them long dead.

Opening the first packet, I was bewildered to find that it contained a beautiful lock of human hair, bound with a silk ribbon. The next packet held more hair, this time scattered inside. The rest of the papers held hair of different lengths and colors, textures and curl. It was a small collection of family hair, nine locks in all, and from the names and dates, it seemed some of it was more than 175 years old. The hair was mostly brown, with one lock of bright blond curls and a couple of others with a reddish tint. A few of the packets had snips of hair, others held locks four inches long. There was one labeled "Aunt Betsy's hair," and another, "WJ Ball's hair—aged 3 years 1824."

I'd wanted an antique, and instead I'd gotten a crypt. Although a strand of hair wasn't a bone, it was a bit of a person, probably the only thing left of them, the rest having turned to dust in the ground. A few of the locks had started to disintegrate, but most had been well preserved in the lightless and airless recesses of the secret drawer, their miniature tomb.

After this surprise, this rendezvous with the deceased, I felt an uncanny presence and a touch of nausea. Out of the laconic desk, an unwelcome aura seemed to have entered the room, the result of my interrupting the sleep of ages. My stomach clenched and my hearing sharpened. That the stash of relics comprised bits of people to whom I was related, whose genes I shared, raised the level of anxiety.

AT THE TIME, I was a resident of Charleston, South Carolina, the old city on the East Coast. After ten years of living in New York, I'd turned my back on the Northeast and returned to the South, the place of my childhood. Charleston at one period had been a commercial engine for the South; but since World War II, it had been content as a tourist destination, desirable for its climate, old houses, and beautiful waterways. People in Charleston thought old belongings were important, and in local fashion I'd bought an old house, in need of work. It was the kind where a plaque on the front says how magnificent was the man who'd built it, centuries ago, even if his name—usually something like Ephraim Codrington, or Nicodemus Leger—sounded like a figure from the Old Testament. All the houses in the neighborhood were old, and people had filled them with old furniture and things they said were old, even when they weren't. An auction place out on the Savannah Highway did good business in such pseudo-antiques. It was surprising how many Regency dressers made in London during Jane Austen's lifetime had washed up in the area, and how some of them looked like young wood beaten with chains.

I was trying to fit in. But assimilation to local ways required certain formulas, such as a love for obsolete opinions, conspicuous patterns of attending church, and skepticism of outsiders, an attitude difficult for an outsider like myself to maintain. I'd outgrown my Southern attributes, if they'd ever existed, during years in colder states, and getting them back felt like trying to wear a suit that was too small.

My father's family lived in Charleston, and they were the main reason I'd come. I had written a couple of books about the South, and I was attempting to rejoin the family group after long separation. My father had been born and raised in Charleston, but he had left his hometown after college. Years later, he'd married my mother, who was from New Orleans. One result of his leaving home was that my brother and I, the only children, fell outside of his family's orbit. We were born in Savannah, Georgia, ninety miles away; admittedly not far, but Charleston is one of those places so happy about its own existence that the rest of the world has been blotted out on all the maps.

After my brother and I could talk, our parents started moving around, until we'd lived in seven places by the time I was eighteen. These were always south of Virginia, and one of them was actually South Carolina, but we stayed just two years. We were itinerants, like Wandering Jews in the South, in a life that made us alien to many of our relatives. Most people in my father's family had spent their lives in Charleston, but I had only returned to it as an adult, like the millions of tourists who come every year to prod the enigma of that old slave city, usually in spring or fall, when it's not so hot that it makes you speechless.

My father died when I was twelve, a suicide, taking his life into his hands after a long illness that involved a brain tumor. The loss of my dad when I was a boy was another reason, in addition to our moving around, that I had a fragile grip on his family. After my father's death, my mother had taken my brother and me back to New Orleans, and for a long time we rarely saw the relatives in South Carolina.

The desk symbolized my return, because, as I said, it was an heirloom. To be a bona fide family member, it helped to have heirlooms, and since I'd never owned any, I went to the trouble of finding some. The many branches of my father's family had picked up a lot of antiques and old things, because this group had been in South Carolina for an unusually long time. The family had been around so long, the general opinion was that if anyone moved away, no one would understand them, and they might just die from exposure. I was a prodigal figure, in a way, and I thought this point of view might be easier for me to handle if I possessed one or two symbols of tradition. Thus, the desk and the other antiques on the delivery truck. Their wood veins, in the mahogany, still ribboned beneath the grime.

I was grown, and I'd moved back. I was married, and owned an old house. I was putting furniture in it. The year was 2000.

I INITIALLY ENCOUNTERED the desk, carrying case for the hair specimens, at the home of an elderly cousin named Jane Gilchrist. Jane had worked for many years in a bookkeeping office at the Charleston Naval Base. She'd been a ballet dancer in her youth, and she'd never married, instead sharing a house with her mother for much of her life. I'd gotten to know Jane—a petite woman, birdlike, quiet from solitude—when she was about sixty-five. Her voice was small and colored with sadness, a wavering dispatch from a lifetime of blocked desire, though we never talked about what alternatives to loneliness Jane might have wanted. Jane pulled her hair back from her face, wore a small range of inexpensive dresses, and withdrew into her 1950s house, the only place I spent time with her.

Despite living in an unassuming subdivision behind a Ford dealership (announcements echoed from the second-hand lot), Jane possessed a large cache of antiques, which

she'd inherited from her mother. Jane's mother had gotten the same furniture from her mother, who'd gotten it from *hers,* a woman named Mary Gibbs Ball. This Mary Ball, Jane's great-grandmother, whom Jane called Greatie, had lived at a place called Limerick plantation, one of many rice farms near Charleston once owned by the Ball family.

Greatie had occupied the big house at Limerick from 1863 until 1891. I know these exact dates because in past years I'd absorbed the history of Jane's and my shared family, and the details have clung to the ganglia of my memory.

My cousin Jane and I had talked about her antiques. When she traced their histories, sometimes Jane repeated what she'd heard from Greatie, sometimes she showed papers that supported what Greatie had said, and occasionally she pulled out nineteenth-century photographs of rooms where the furniture could be seen in its original setting, within a plantation house.

Limerick plantation, twenty-five miles north of Charleston, was a place to which we both traced roots—or, perhaps I should say genes. Jane's great-grandfather, William James Ball, had owned the place. Jane was descended from this man's second wife, Mary Gibbs (Greatie), and I from his first, a woman named Julia Cart. In genetic terms, William James Ball was the person in whom Jane's and my DNA commingled. He was also the person who'd contributed the earliest lock of hair to the collection, the one labeled "WJ Ball's hair—aged 3 years 1824."

When William Ball died, in 1891, Limerick plantation was sold, and the contents of the house went to Jane's great-grandmother, Greatie. After Greatie's death, the same belongings went to her daughter, and afterward to her daughter, then to that woman's daughter, who was Jane.

Among the oddments handed down was an early barometer, an instrument dating from the 1850s and consisting of a glass hemisphere that covered a pipette filled with mercury. It looked like one of the magical things Thomas Jefferson had built for pleasure and utility at Monticello. As a planter, William Ball had used the barometer to predict rain, to help him decide when to irrigate. The barometer may also have been a fancy toy he showed off to the men in the neighborhood, other plantation owners.

Jane possessed pocket watches and mechanical pencils, things once owned by family members in the 1800s, and she had leather-bound books signed by some of them. Her lore about her collection was credible, and she made clear that all the antiques had moved down through the generations together, like a bolus through a snake. She pointed out how her things had occupied a single household at the beginning, and how they'd come to rest in her own. The unity of her belongings—the critical mass of the furniture, eight or nine pieces from the early 1800s, plus the personal possessions—made a preponderance of evidence that the original home of Jane's collected goods had indeed been Limerick plantation.

One thing she had was the old desk, or secretary, which she said had at one time been used as "the plantation office." It was during January when I first saw the desk, and it stood in an unheated cinderblock room where the temperature ran about thirty degrees. The desk was dirty and sagging. I didn't know about the hidden compartment then, and Jane didn't show it to me. She might not have known about it either.

I moved away from Charleston, and during that time my cousin Jane died, at age seventy, of cancer. I heard about the funeral while in New York. A few months later, Jane's will bequeathed her house and its contents to one of her brothers; but this heir had no room for dilapidated tables and chairs. I belonged to a dangling branch of the family, and not the main trunk. So I offered Jane's brother $10,000 for the desk and other pieces. Money moves things around, even in the Old South.

THE DESK NEEDED attention, and to put it right, I hired a cabinetmaker named David Beckford, who restored eighteenth-century furniture for museums. A thin, handsome man in his forties, David had dark hair, a New England accent, and an abstract manner. Considerable silences separated his words. He knew tea tables and sideboards like his fingernails, however, because he'd apprenticed in the restoration rooms of antiques dealers, a drudgery that had left him a purist. At our first meeting, David said he wouldn't restore furniture made after 1830, his doomsday date for when factory production drove out the last handcraftsmen.

According to this antiques doctor, or restoration cabinetmaker, the desk had probably been built between 1790 and 1810, in Charleston. He based his estimate on details of the construction, like its joints and type of wood. David also said the plain design of the secretary hadn't been suited to the front rooms of a house; that it had probably been a back-office desk, fit for business and money (which helped explain the hidden compartment). He took the things apart and found neither markings nor a signature that would identify its maker, which he said was unsurprising, because many cabinetmakers at the time didn't see their work as art to be signed.

Art and antiques dealers talk about the provenance of an

object, a record of who has owned something and how this might be proved. Provenance is equivalent to chain of custody in criminal law, which tracks evidence from crime scene to trial. And after the hair surfaced, the antique desk struck me as a kind of courtroom exhibit.

Account books kept by family members from the period had survived, and these belonged to various libraries, but I couldn't find reference to the old desk in any of them. Nevertheless, circumstantial evidence pointed to a man named Elias Ball III as the person who had commissioned the secretary from a cabinetmaker around 1790. Elias Ball III was a bald, fat, and rich planter of rice who'd lived through the Revolution and had never married. Old wills associated the desk with him, and family tradition said the secretary had spent its first century or so at Limerick plantation, which had once been his. Elias Ball III owned Limerick between 1786, when he inherited it and moved in, and his death a quarter of a century later. It would have made sense for him to acquire a new desk soon after taking charge of the place, to organize his deal-making.

The desk's presumptive first owner was a lifelong bachelor and spendthrift socialite who'd lived high and suffered from gout. When Elias Ball III died in 1810, at age fifty-eight, his estate passed to his nephew, Isaac Ball, who inherited the plantation, its enslaved people, and the house. It was this man, Isaac Ball, along with his wife, Eliza Poyas Ball, who had actually started the hair collection. But it would take time to discover this, and to understand why.

THE PACKETS OF HAIR came out from their clandestine place and went into plastic bags. During the month after they surfaced, each time I looked at the bits of paper, I saw a different meaning. Initially, the hair collection made me think of fingerprints, evidence of a forgotten crime; another time, it was a morbid expression of Victorian style. During the 1800s, people made jewelry from hair, putting strands of it into gold lockets and weaving rings and bracelets from long locks. The hair collection differed from this, however, because you couldn't wear this stuff, and it wasn't decorated up. The hidden drawer didn't strike me as a jewelry box as much as it did a natural history cabinet: its contents were like fossils, or teeth, little extras Louis and Mary Leakey might have kept on the mantel.

I've noticed while getting a haircut that they're quick to sweep up the cuttings. I take this to mean that customers are not happy to see their hair lying out on the floor. You especially don't like to see several haircuts mixed up in a pile. Hair carries a morsel of one's being, and cut hair is a reminder of mortality. Thus my discovery released fitful emotions, like those that might go with finding a dead mouse in a dresser drawer. In the strange companionship of these hair samples, and as a rational person with no taste for the occult, I admit that I had a feeling of visitation, a sense of reanimation of the dead.

Finally the hair went into a box, so I wouldn't have to deal with it. The spectral feeling went away, replaced with questions. Who were the people who'd stored their locks in tiny time capsules? Why did they collect hair, as they might have arranged pictures? And what, if anything, did it mean?

Obviously, I couldn't get answers, because the owners of the hair were gone. Or were they?

NOT LONG AFTER the packets had come out of hiding, my mother died, at age eighty-three. My brother and I laid her to rest in New Orleans, in the aboveground tomb of her family in that place. Then came an aftershock, the seismic settling that occurs when both of your parents are gone. If your parents have died, along with grief, and fear, and a sense of taking-their-place, you feel you have to realign your memories. Your early years look like an uncertain dream, because you can no longer share the utopia of your childhood (an idyll, even if it was a mess). Where are the reference points? Who is left to please?

A little after my mother died, I took out the hair from the box in which it had languished. The hair consisted of bits of relatives, making it attractive as surrogate intimacy. And, this time, after a few viewings of the locks, I couldn't get the things out of my mind.

I put on gloves and picked up the folded paper labeled "WJ Ball's hair—aged 3 years 1824." William James Ball, my father's great-grandfather. His hair was soft and brown, as curly as the morning it left his head. I felt a little ashamed handling it, the uneasiness an archaeologist must feel after shoveling up a grave. I hoped I wouldn't have descendants who fingered my remains.

The little boy's hair in hand, it occurred to me that I carried some of his genes. Next to him was a folded piece of paper labeled, "Isaac Ball, aged 4 yrs," and another marked simply "John Ball." Sprinkles of their genes, too, and some from all the others. The relatives remained quiet in their little packets, passengers on a train through time. And a question took shape: Was there DNA in the hair? Or certain chemicals, evidence of how they'd died?

To forensics, a family is not a furnace of love and drama, as it feels from the inside. It's a box of evidence: DNA samples, fingerprints, hair. A lot of people in this family had died young: the sample labeled, "John Ball, b1825 d1852," came from a man who died at twenty-six, leaving a wife and two children. This John Ball had had a brother who died at six and a sister who died at four. Toxicology and chemistry might have something to say about this. And molecular biology. During the 1990s, DNA science had become the big storyteller in forensics. And since the completion of the Human Genome Project, in 2003, molecular biology had also mobbed family stories. To most of the public, it no longer seems strange that genes are the web that connects families, and that people are like attachments to the network, merely expressions of their DNA.

One often hears of DNA in miraculous terms, like the trace on the cigarette butt that sends the guy to jail. The Pentagon takes a sample from new soldiers, in case one encounters a roadside bomb and the Armed Forces DNA Identification Laboratory must confirm a soldier's identity. A national awareness of trace evidence and genes sharpened after September 11, 2001, when the families of World Trade Center victims carried toothbrushes and combs to the New York medical examiner's office, and lab workers tried to match human tissue from Ground Zero with DNA from cheek cells and hair.

This uncomfortable memory, an image that stunned at the time, answered the forensic question about the presence of DNA in the hair collection. If the 9/11 families had used hairbrush tangles as testing material, then the desk hair might have DNA in it, or traces of other compounds. And if that DNA could be extracted, what had surfaced from the hidden compartment was not just the product of some bad antebellum haircuts, but an unsolved forensic case.

FOR NOW, THE HAIR was a bunch of characters. The one marked "John Ball, b1825 d1852" was a reddish-brown strand, two inches long, and the name fit with what I knew about a long-gone cousin. This John Ball had been the youngest of four children, but he hadn't known his father, Isaac Ball, a man I've mentioned, who had died of malaria three months after John's birth. John Ball was a skinny boy who, although fatherless, nevertheless grew up with luxuries, an education, two houses, and a trip to Europe when he was a teenager. A portrait of him survives in the collection of a museum in Charleston, a palm-sized miniature done when he was in his early twenties. It shows him to have been a beautiful brown-eyed man, with sharp cheekbones and thick eyebrows, a perfect isosceles triangle of a nose, and thick hair parted on the right. At age twenty-one, in 1846, John Ball had married one of his cousins, a woman named Maria Gibbs. At that time, it was not unusual for cousins to marry. The couple had had two children, plus a third who would die as an infant. With the big exception of the baby, things had been all right for John and Maria. But in his mid-twenties, John Ball died, leaving a widow and two children, the oldest a boy of four. The hair, dated the year of his death, seems to have been cut during his final illness.

The other strands also had stories. "Isaac Ball, aged 4 yrs" was a little boy who would eventually run a rice plantation with black sharecroppers and have twelve children. And then there was "Aunt Betsy's hair." The lock from her folded scrap of paper had belonged to a measurably strange and endearing woman.

Aunt Betsy, an aunt of the person who had started the hair collection, had been a woman named Elizabeth Anne Scott Poyas. Born in 1792, she was the first child of Richard and Harriet Scott, who owned rice plantations near Charleston. Aunt Betsy's mother, Harriet, seems to have been the one in her marriage with the money, which Aunt Betsy's father had gotten his hands on when he married. I discovered little about Aunt Betsy's childhood, but she married at around age twenty, that being about the highest age a woman with a dowry could expect to reach and still keep suitors away from her cash. Aunt Betsy had raised several children, but in middle age her life changed, because she started to write.

In the Old South, for a woman to write anything more than letters was regarded as unseemly, antisocial. But beginning in her fifties, Aunt Betsy published four books, as well as frequent newspaper pieces. Her subject was South Carolina "society," a word she used to refer to her own circle, people with property, mainly plantation owners. In 1853, she published her first book, *A Peep Into the Past*. It was a protracted gossip column about the Carolina rich—their names, doings, and (infrequently) their mistakes. Aunt Betsy's style was chatty and flattering, with digressive sentences about who had been married to whom, under what circumstances, people's funny habits, and what they'd done that was worth remembering. Two years after her first book, she published *The Olden Time of Carolina, by the Octogenarian Lady of Charleston,* another gossipy exercise. Unlike modern gossip, Aunt Betsy's wasn't cruel. In fact, she fawned over her subjects. The author took a nostalgic view of the early 1800s, the time of her youth, and she seemed to want to show that America had been in decline since the country had expanded beyond the Appalachians; that only "society" was preserving the old values. Aunt Betsy was sixty-three when she called herself "the Octogenarian Lady," a conceit that probably helped her get past objections to women who wrote. Her lock of hair looks like it might have been dyed.

THE HAIR WAS a group of people, and I had the idea to use it to investigate them. What would forensic examiners look for in hair? DNA, certainly. Traces of other things, residues.

I wasn't sure DNA could enhance family stories, but I did know that genetics might throw light on one thing, and that was the matter of our origins. My mother's family, as well as my father's, both prided themselves on their roots. My father's branch is said to have come from England, and my mother's, maybe half, from France. Many Americans take their lineage for granted, content with a few pieces of lore.

The families of my parents have never done this. We know, or we think we know, everything of interest that has happened to everyone among us, going back as far as the first immigrants. For example, we would say that my mother's family, whose surname is Rowley, became Southerners precisely in 1834, when a New Yorker with an eye for the main chance named Charles N. Rowley, wandering out of an unexceptional family from Vermont, met a rich widow from Mississippi, Jane Kemp Girault, as she was vacationing near Rochester on a "mourning trip" after her husband's death. Charles Rowley married Jane Girault and moved with her to Mississippi, where he took possession of her deceased husband's cotton plantation, Marengo, and seventy-six enslaved farmhands. Subsequent Rowleys moved on to Louisiana and have lived for a long time in New Orleans.

We know, or we say we know, our deepest identity. Put bluntly, we know that we're thoroughly white. This kind of thing used to be important among Southern families, until it became unacceptable to discuss; removed from the table, it hasn't diminished in importance very much. The chronicles tell us there are no Jews, blacks, Latinos, Asians, Arabs, or Native Americans in our historical mix. But the chronicles contain hearsay, and the records have gaps. People hide things. Could genetic tests tell us what we really are, historically speaking, in a verifiable, scientific sense?

OBSESSION CREPT INTO my office. I began to inspect the hair like a lab technician (not only gloves, but tweezers). I went to libraries to read periodicals like the *Journal of Foren-*

sic Sciences. I discovered that where forensic literature might lack style, it had jargon. (Sample article title: "Genomewide Linkage Scan for Myopia Susceptibility Loci among Ashkenazi Jewish Families Shows Evidence of Linkage on Chromosome 22q12.")

Forensics used to involve fingerprints and chalk outlines of bodies, but these practices have moved to the background, like fedoras on detectives. The correct setting for criminalistics is often less the crime scene than a lab bench, and the proper vocabulary, "buccal swabs," "extraction and sequencing," "microsatellites," "haplotypes," and "single-nucleotide polymorphisms."

Family memory is what grandparents say about the past, and maybe what people write in their diaries. The hair collection promised to be a new type of chronicle. It offered a set of fresh recollections, raw material for a genetic memoir.

2 *The Molecule*

To judge from the reverence with which people talk about it, deoxyribonucleic acid is a mystical, quasi-religious substance. It doesn't require much time with a television to see how entertainment and news media love DNA, which appears like the vanquishing hero in documentaries and fiction, movies and print, in scene-stealing roles. The miraculous deeds of the molecule can vary: it's the key to crime stories, unlocking the ending and naming the villain; it's the master code of medicine, promising to heal (if the codebreakers can decrypt it). It's the voice of evolution, revealing events of 100,000 years ago, before humans walked out of Africa to people the rest of the world. Not immune to the magic of DNA, I had expectations of the hair collection. Would the genetic data in the hair tell new family stories, or spill old medical secrets?

Deoxyribonucleic acid is a molecule, and genes, merely segments of it. A gene isn't a pellet or a granule, but tens of thousands of nucleotides in a stretch of a given chromosome. Imagine a single molecule of DNA to be like a long piece of movie film, the celluloid that runs through a projector, and imagine that every frame corresponds to a single nucleotide. Genes are like scenes in the movie. At twenty-four frames per second, a projector runs through 1,440 frames for each minute of screen time. A functioning gene would be a coherent fifteen-minute scene followed by a half-hour of nonsense flicker ("junk DNA"); the next gene, a ten-minute scene, then an hour and a half of garble, and so on. The physical object of the film, held in the hand, would look nearly the same, but the difference would be apparent during projection.

The strands of DNA are vastly long, and you have to look at them at individual sites, in close-up. The strip of celluloid might reach from Paris to London, and to study it, you pick up the film at some point in the English Channel and peer with a magnifying glass. A site on the DNA molecule is a "locus," the specific physical location of a gene or variation, its whereabouts. A marker, or genetic signpost, appears at a given locus.

"Gene expression" is what genetics calls the making of a person. Consider an embryo, which has two complete sets of chromosomes, forty-six molecules of DNA, in every cell. One set of chromosomes comes from each parent, though its contents have been shuffled prior to conception, making it similar to but not a copy of the mother's or father's DNA. At each gene location, the DNA in paired chromosomes might be the same, or it might possess alternative forms, different genes for, say, finger length. The two gene possibilities (long or short fingers) are called "alleles" (it's pronounced *ah-leal*). One allele for every gene is inherited from each parent. The two alleles might convey the same instruction, or they might code for differing characteristics. Things can go this way or that. If the alleles differ, when the gene sets come together in the human egg, one of the genes (nucleotides controlling finger length) can override the other. The gene that controls the outcome is said to be dominant over the gene that doesn't, which is recessive. One genetic result is expressed in the embryo, monopolizing finger length thereafter.

When two individuals possess two different alleles of a gene, the variation in DNA sequence is a "polymorphism" (more than one version: *poly* = many, *morph* = shape). Polymorphisms can be sorted to glimpse the instructions of specific genes. Suppose at a given locus a woman has one type of gene for pendulous earlobes, and it sits next to a gene for highly arched eyebrows. Another person might have a polymorphic version of those genes. She might possess a gene for short earlobes next to one for flat eyebrows. If short earlobes and flat eyebrows occur throughout the second woman's family, those two genes are said to be "linked." Genes are linked when they occur close enough together on a chromosome that the probability they will be separated during the preconception gene shuffling is low; and therefore, the probability they will be inherited together is high. Linkage analysis is the attempt to sort the frequency of polymorphisms, how they are arranged together, and whether they travel from one generation to another in clusters.

The word chromosome means "colored body" (Greek: *chroma* = color, *soma* = body). It appeared a century ago, when chemists first stained them with solutions to make them colored bodies that showed up under a microscope. Chromosomes are DNA, artfully compressed and packaged; they are the luggage that carries the genes. If unwound, DNA might resemble a seemingly endless strand or dribble, like a combination of all the drips in a big Jackson Pollock painting. As it is, human DNA is bunched into a set of chromosomes. Proteins called histones act like spools, and DNA winds around them to form beads on a string, and the beaded string winds upon itself, tier upon tier, to form the clumps in the familiar photographs. The nucleotide chain is in there, but no degree of magnification can show it. The human genome comes in two parts, half from each parent. Altogether in the nucleus of a cell, you have forty-six chromosomes. They consist of twenty-two pairs of "autosomes," which are like the regular fuel, and one pair of high-octane—the sex chromosomes, X and Y. Chromosomes become visible during the minutes of cell division (mitosis). Each chromosome (23 x 2 = 46 chromosomes per cell) makes a copy of itself, so that for a brief period you have ninety-two of them crammed in a nucleus. As the cell divides, the DNA contracts and bunches up in a tidy way, which is the moment it becomes visible. Each chromosome then splits from its copy, and identical groups of chromosomes migrate to opposite ends of the cell, getting out of the way of each other for the breach. Two cells appear where there had been one, and it's back to forty-six chromosomes in each cell, invisible again.

Mitosis happens everywhere in the body, millions of times an hour, with exact copies of the chromosomes produced pretty much every time. Things really count in meiosis, which is cell division within the ovaries or testes. If you looked inside a testicle at the part that makes sperm, you'd find about 200,000 compartments (not that you'd count), each of which contains a meandering tube, or seminiferous tubule. Within the tubes, parent cells make the raw material of sperm, so-called primary spermatocytes, cells with forty-six chromosomes, like ordinary cells. But after their genesis, these spermatocytes divide in a way no other body cells can. (A parallel process takes place in ovaries.)

During this division, meiosis, the chromosomes duplicate themselves, but they add a further stage, recombination. The twinned chromosomes line up into flowerlike, four-handed figures. At this point the chromosomes "recombine," randomly exchanging fragments of themselves with each other in a choreography that can be seen with a microscope. Recombination is the roulette spin of genes, the point where natural selection stirs things to create variety. After the exchange of genetic material, the twinned chromosomes pull apart and the spermatocyte divides into two, so that it generates two cells, each with a different mix of genes. And the shakedown continues. Within the two new cells, the forty-six chromosomes of the nucleus split into two sets of twenty-three. The two cells divide again, but now each new cell ends up with only one of these abbreviated groups. In the end are four cells, each with half the usual number of chromosomes, and because of recombination, the genetic material in all of them differs. In women, one of these four cells matures to become an ovum; in men, all four can become the familiar spermatozoan with the big head and wiggling tail.

Despite the sound of its language, which can be precious, molecular biology is not an occult practice. It might be better to call it a trade. DNA science compares to the construction industry. Just as carpenters apprentice to experienced builders, learning the things that go into buildings (sash, stud, rafter) and the ways they're joined (mortised, mortared, bolted), DNA scientists are contractors of the molecule, who learn how it's put together. They apprentice in a lab to manipulate genetic material, after which they have trouble talking to noncarpenters.

Science journalists are prone to treat DNA as though everything in people might be read in their genes—football skill, heart disease, ambition, fingernail strength, altruism, alcoholism, social ease, obesity, sex choices, risk of depression, the likelihood of Alzheimer's. To read the reports, there is nothing hidden to genetic analysis, because there is nothing deeper than genes, nothing "beneath" them.

These, at any rate, are the talking points from the technological news stream. The real DNA molecule turns out to be blander, its powers more crude.

FORENSICS STARTS IN a lab, and after a brief search I found Mitotyping Technologies, in Pennsylvania, a company whose only job was to extract DNA from hair. Law enforcement agencies crowded the lab's client list, from the

FBI to small-town police departments with an officer force in the single digits. Each client had the same thing: hairs from a criminal case, meticulously labeled. Each sent them by overnight mail, and each got an analysis.

I brought my specimens by hand. Mitotyping Technologies occupies a converted physician's office in the small city of State College, Pennsylvania, in the geographic center of that state. The 40,000 students of State College, associated with Pennsylvania State University, overshadow the 40,000 year-round residents, especially on football days, when the screaming from Beaver Stadium bounces off nearby Nittany Mountain.

A woman answers the door and locks it behind. "We're careful not to have any DNA coming in or flying out that we don't know about," she says.

Terry Melton is trim, in her fifties, with short brown hair streaked in blond highlights. She wears black jeans with a cowboy belt and a black-and-white striped turtleneck, and her manner is friendly, chamber of commerce style. She says she started the company in 1998, and, as a woman doing science, she'd found it easy to borrow the money.

"We do human hairs that are naturally shed that are found at crime scenes," Melton says. "For example, a hair found in the hand of a victim during a violent struggle, or a foreign pubic hair where the perpetrator has worn a condom and there is no semen to do nuclear testing."

The name, Mitotyping Technologies, refers to the type of DNA in hair. Melton says she explains it to juries all the time. Two varieties of the molecule occur in the body: nuclear DNA, which exists in every cell nucleus, and is the

DNA that mothers and fathers convey to children; and mitochondrial DNA, which appears outside the nucleus, and which only comes from the mother. These facts bear on the hair specimens, because during formation in the follicle, nuclear DNA is removed from hair, leaving only mitochondrial DNA. Which meant that I would be able to ask some questions of the hair samples, and not others.

Lab technicians write it as mtDNA, and I would hear one or two refer to it as "mite." Mitochondrial DNA exists inside tiny, peanut-shaped mitochondria, thousands in each cell; mitochondria control respiration, producing energy for cell function. They're said to be the remnants of parasites, bacteria from the evolutionary past that became useful to their human hosts. Invaders that turned into houseguests, and stayed for a billion years.

MtDNA and nuclear DNA (nuDNA) possess the same chemical structure, but the mitochondrial kind is much smaller. It also conveys differently, as I said, passing down the female line alone. Children carry the mitochondrial signature that was present in their mother's egg, because the mitochondria in sperm cells are destroyed after fertilization.

The line of questioning also differs. Because of its matrilineal path, mtDNA only carries information about one's mother's family (and one's maternal grandmother, great-grandmother, and so on). This meant I wouldn't be able to say whether the people in the hair collection had had Duchenne muscular dystrophy, but I might be able to say something else, such as whether any of them had once had family in Africa.

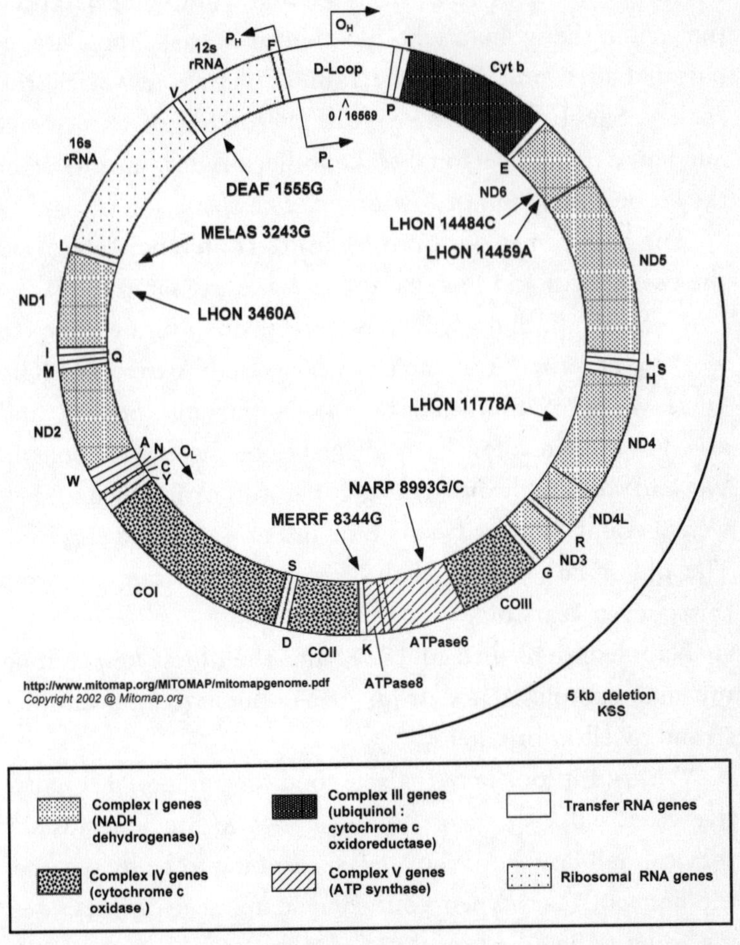

Mitochondrial DNA, the type of DNA present in hair, is 16,569 nucleotides in length (compared with 2.8 billion in nuclear DNA) and is diagrammed as a circular structure rather than a linear one. It contains a section 1,123 nucleotides in length called the "displacement loop," or "D-loop," where the order of nucleotides changes often, that is, every few thousand years.

At Mitotyping Technologies, I give Terry Melton the sample labeled "Aunt Betsy's hair." Aunt Betsy had been the writer, the woman who nicknamed herself "the Octogenarian Lady" and published four books about Charleston society. She'd regarded herself as the orchid of refinement. She had as much personal stake in her origins, and whether they'd been way up, or low down, as anyone.

The hair comes out onto Melton's conference table, and she uses gloves and forceps to open the first sample.

"I think the hairs you have are probably not going to work," she says. "You can't always get DNA from old hair. Once we were contacted by the Napoleonic Society and asked to analyze a few hairs alleged to be those of Napoleon. We had absolutely no luck getting stuff from them. They were a couple hundred years old, and no DNA had survived. The oldest hairs we've had success with in our lab were thirty-seven years old."

Napoleon had died in 1821, and the oldest hair among my nine samples dated from 1824. But tweezing another strand, Melton brightens.

"Neat-o! It looks pretty darn good for a hundred seventy-five years old," she says. "Nice, glossy. My technicians say they can tell how hard the analysis is going to be by whether the hair collapses when you grind it up. If it disintegrates, it's going to be a bad result."

Terry Melton had been born and raised in Charlottesville, Virginia, and her speech retained the imprint of that state. She'd raised two children and then, in her thirties, gone to Penn State for a PhD in genetics. Melton said she'd never seen a similar collection of hair and added that her relatives in Virginia would admire it. "It's a Southern thing," she says. "My grandmother had a desk in her house in Virginia Beach that had a secret drawer in it."

Forensics requires an obsessive turn, a trait conspicuous in hair analysis. "I think sometimes I have a kind of sickness," Melton says. "I go into public restrooms, and I see a hair, and I say to myself, 'There's a nice big one by the sink, and maybe I should take it!' "

Melton points out that obsession is not hers alone, because clients also bring attitudes. "One man claimed to have collected hair from Bigfoot," she says. Melton says she told the man that she couldn't analyze Bigfoot's hairs, because her testing protocol was human-specific. "I said, 'How do we know what kind of DNA Bigfoot has?' "

Mitotyping Technologies also examines bone for DNA content, old murder cases being the main source of samples. This led one client to come forward with the skull of an alien. "He wanted me to take out the extraterrestrial DNA," Melton says. "It turned out to be a nine-hundred-year-old dysmorphic child's skull that had been found in Mexico."

The first step in analyzing the hair collection would be to try to get DNA from it. This wouldn't be easy, per the Napoleon example. If it could be done, Melton says, the DNA was likely to be a very small amount, and damaged by age. The second stage would be to sequence this sample, detail the order of its nucleotides. This, too, would be complicated by the nature of old DNA. One could only ask questions after this sequencing data had come in.

Forensics is said to be the application of science to legal questions (Latin, *forensis* = of the forum, or public space). The noun has no singular; it takes the permanent-plural of scientific style, which derives *physics* from the Latin *physica* (study of nature). The job of parsing forensic evidence arose in the Victorian decades, when police acquired uniforms, budgets, and a desire to transcend their role as municipal gangs. They turned to new fields, like photography and microscopy.

One of the earliest police laboratories opened in Los Angeles, in 1924. (President Theodore Roosevelt had established the Federal Bureau of Investigation in 1908, and the FBI lab dates from 1932.) New York City first appointed a medical examiner—a pathologist who performs autopsies and pronounces on cause of demise—in 1918, and afterward autopsies became routine, spreading from murder victims to natural deaths. A guild, the American Academy of Forensic Sciences, came in 1948, then the trade periodicals, such as *Science and Justice* and the *Journal of Forensic Sciences.*

Hair analysis has survived an uneven reputation since its introduction as a forensic specialty. In 1884, William J. Lewis, a microscope enthusiast from Buffalo, published a twenty-page paper, "Hair: microscopically examined and medico-legally considered," which he'd presented at a microscope convention. Lewis seems to have been the originator of hair forensics. But only some courtrooms have favored hair, because hairs look alike, even to educated eyes. Since DNA testing, hair evidence has become more reliable, and the credibility of hair experts has risen.

Prior to DNA, forensics involved much evidence of a masculine cast—bullets, explosives, guns, tool marks. DNA changed that, shouldering aside experts who'd memorized differences between tire treads. Since the creation of genetic databases, the center of gravity for criminalistics has moved from the gun range to the lab bench. Small-town police officers take seminars on the handling of cheek swabs and fret over online modules about types of genetic markers. Gloves, delicacy, meticulousness: the protocol in crime-solving has been feminized.

A British-born academic named Alec Jeffreys may be more responsible for these developments than any other individual. For his creation, "DNA fingerprinting," Alec Jeffreys, a geneticist at the University of Leicester, in central England, has been knighted, won the Einstein Award, been given a lifetime salary by the Royal Society (the British scientific academy, founded 1660), and inducted into the National Inventors Hall of Fame, a tiny club in America whose members include the man who originated the photocopier. Forensic examiners regard Alec Jeffreys, a blunt and private man, as the Moses who led them from the low valley of footprint analysis to the high plain of DNA matching, a giddy ascent. Quite by accident, Jeffreys has made a hero of the diffident lab tech, the biology graduate whose alchemy links the suspect to the scene.

During the early 1980s, Alec Jeffreys was studying DNA variation between people and had the thought to inspect short pieces of genetic material, on the premise that no individual would have exactly the same eight or nine chromosome shards as another. He identified a bit of DNA called a “minisatellite,” a repetitive section whose sequence reads like a short phrase that recurs dozens of times. Comparing several minisatellites, Jeffreys saw that people possessed slight sequence differences, which could be read and cataloged.

The British patent on DNA fingerprinting dates from Jeffreys's initial publication on the subject, “Hypervariable ‘Minisatellite’ Regions in Human DNA,” in a 1985 issue of *Nature*. The U.S. registration came ten years later, after revisions, as patent number 5,413,908.

After the method became widespread, around 1990, forensics acquired a mass of data and institutions to manage it. The chief criminal genetic database in the United States, operational since 1998 and run by the FBI, is the Combined DNA Index System, or CODIS. It's said to be “combined” because it links several types of data: state and federal criminal records, DNA profiles of convicted criminals, and profiles from evidence taken at crime scenes. When designing CODIS, the FBI decided on a template, a profile system of thirteen genetic markers spread over twelve chromosomes. (Whereas Alec Jeffreys had looked at minisatellites, CODIS looks at smaller bits of DNA, called “microsatellites.”) The likelihood that two samples might share the same profile, the same thirteen microsatellites, was regarded as a statistical impossibility (except in the case of identical twins, who carry the same DNA).

All states require samples from felons, and all load DNA profiles into CODIS. The genetic profiles of 2.5 million people appear in the digital bank, a number to be dwarfed as new samples come online. Blood and semen provide the majority of profiles, but hair has also come along, feeding mitochondrial data into separate databases.

With CODIS, DNA seeped to the roots of enforcement, and its power has fertilized new agencies, fresh surveillance. In 2001, during panic about anthrax in the mails, the FBI created "microbial forensics," opening a lab at Fort Dietrich, Maryland, to sequence the genomes of viruses and write scenarios for biological sabotage. Other applications of DNA to crime, whether real or anticipated, will inevitably be hatched.

JOHANN FRIEDRICH MIESCHER was a twenty-five-year-old Swiss introvert who suffered a serious hearing impairment. In 1868, he had gotten his medical degree in Switzerland, but the hearing trouble and shyness made him averse to patient contact. Miescher wanted to do lab work, and so moved to Germany to study chemistry at the university in Tübingen. At his bench, Miescher inspected cell nuclei, hitherto mysterious, but now visible under the microscope, hoping to determine what they contained. His experiments involved pus-soaked bandages taken from a local clinic, a disgusting business in which Miescher would salvage gauze from trash bins and wash out the ooze to get material. Pus contains white blood cells, which have large nuclei and little cytoplasm, and the shy doctor found a way to get the nucleus out of those cells undamaged. He tried different reactions on the nuclei, until one procedure left an unusual, pale precipitate. The residue behaved differently from other organic substances, because it resisted the enzyme pepsin, which ate through most bio-matter. He called it "nuclein," but he couldn't guess its function. Years later, Miescher extracted a purer form of nuclein, a stringy, white goo (this time, out of Rhine salmon), which one of his students renamed "nucleic acid," because it tested acidic. The substance was DNA, deoxyribonucleic acid, although it would be seventy-five years before it acquired its unpronounceable name.

Horace Freeland Judson's *The Eighth Day of Creation: Makers of the Revolution in Biology* is a history of DNA science and a beautiful piece of writing (if a 700-page text is a "piece"). Some things here about molecular biology, such as the facts about Miescher, have been borrowed from Judson, and also some of the science.

The example of Johann Miescher shows that DNA had been around labs for a long time before two researchers at Cambridge, Francis Crick and James Watson, puzzled out how it looked as a molecule. But no one believed nucleic acid was "the genetic material" until the 1940s.

A nucleic acid has three parts: a sugar called ribose, made from five carbon atoms in the shape of a pentagon; a second part, a phosphate consisting of a phosphorous atom ringed by four oxygen atoms; and a last bit, a "base," made for the most part from nitrogen and carbon atoms. The raw materials of DNA. The three components (ribose, phosphate, base) together make a nucleotide, which is L-shaped and which sockets together with other nucleotides to form one side of the ladderlike DNA molecule. On the other side are more L-shaped nucleotides, flipped over and running in the opposite direction. The two superlong sides are connected in the middle of each ladder rung, which is like a flat step with a joint in the center. The connected bases are called base pairs. Total human DNA is close to three billion base pairs. (The National Center for Biotechnology Information, part of the National Institutes of Health, consolidating the results of the Human Genome Project, puts the number at 2,834,950,000.)

These adaptable parts (ribose, phosphate, base) actually make two kinds of nucleic acid: *ribo*nucleic acid (RNA) and *deoxy*ribonucleic acid (DNA). The latter gets its name because the ribose sugar is missing an oxygen atom, which gives you the mouth-garbling prefix *de-oxy.* DNA is the more-or-less permanent molecule.

DNA opereates like a chemical text where the body writes itself down to remember itself. It doesn't happen just a single time, in utero, but throughout life; when you have a cut, the repair function refers to the skin-making genes to execute the suture. Meanings and instructions appear in the order of the bases. Four different types of bases comprise the DNA chain: *guanine, adenine, cytosine,* and *thymine*, abbreviated in the literature as *G, A, C,* and *T.* Guanine takes its name from bird droppings, because it was isolated in guano in 1844. It consists of two linked rings formed of nitrogen and carbon, to which two spurs or additional atoms are attached. Adenine resembles guanine in its structure, with slight differences. The two other bases, thymine and cytosine, are made of one little ring, which includes nitrogen and carbon, with spurs at the edges that distinguish them from each other. In RNA, a fifth base, uracil is switched for thymine, and occupies the same place as thymine in the DNA template from which RNA is formed. Most high school students know that the bases have rules of combination. Guanine (one side of the ladder rung) pairs with cytosine (other side), thymine with adenine. A base pair is merely one unit, such as a guanine on one side joined to a cytosine on the other side. Chromosome 3, one of the larger ones, contains 199,411,731 base pairs. When DNA shifts to message mode, it generates an RNA twin that consists of an inversion, like a photonegative. The sequence G-A-C-T becomes C-U-G-A (the U being uracil). As the nucleotides tap out their bulletins in an alphabet of four letters, DNA behaves like Morse Code. (Better to put it the other way around: Morse Code behaves like DNA.)

In 1961, Francis Crick was able to show how the order of nucleotides encodes messages, giving instruction to the organism about creating proteins, the constituents of tissue. Bodies contain a bewildering number of proteins, but each can be disassembled into its component amino acids. There are twenty amino acids, which in the right formations (cadets in a drill) make the stipulated protein (muscle, hair, stomach lining). The task of DNA is to call out the names of amino acids and tell them how to assemble.

It was soon demonstrated that the code for this roll call is based on the number three. Three bases stand for a single amino acid. Among the sixty-four possible triplet combinations that can be made from the four bases, sixty-one of them encode one or another of the twenty amino acids, and three of them function as start and stop signs, telling protein-building to get going, or if finished, to shut down. Crick gave a quirky name to the rules of protein design, "the Central Dogma," giving it a somewhat Stalinist connotation. The Central Dogma dictates that information moves in one direction only, from DNA toward protein, and not the reverse. Proteins cannot tell DNA how to assemble.

DNA is the same molecule in all life, mollusks and men, women and wallabies. The word *genome*, a recent coinage, merely means the complete sequence of bases that code for a specific organism, a species script. The human genome may have 2.8 billion base pairs, but a typical estimate has it that only one in twenty of them instruct any activity in the body. The rest are the infamous "junk DNA"—a bad name, since these long stretches include remnants of life from millions of years of evolution. Here are genes left by washed-up viruses that implanted themselves a thousand generations ago, or garbled code for the wings of the flying lemurs that humans once were. It's not junk, so much as a record of what's been lived, a bunch of scripts secreted away and taking up space, like old systems files on a hard drive.

About half the human genome (already ten times the script required to make a person) consists of segments left by old viruses that invaded human predecessors and got themselves copied into the DNA of a population. Suppose an epidemic of viral meningitis struck in the Congo estuary 75,000 years ago, and the survivors, who were infected but resistant, passed the viral genes to their descendants (in other words, to the current world population). One form of old viruses consists of Long Interspersed Nuclear Elements (LINEs), which are leftover retroviruses. (The name retrovirus comes from their behavior; their genomes are made of RNA, and they reverse their composition to make DNA copies of themselves, in order to insert their footprint into the host.) LINEs run to about six thousand bases in length. Another type of left-behind material, SINEs (Short Interspersed Nuclear Elements), are segments 100–400 bases in length that always appear on the tail of a LINE. The most studied of these is the *Alu* insertion, a genomic parasite so common that it makes up 11 percent of the human genome.

We're nearing the end of the esoteric material on DNA, and I regret that some of it might have been opaque. In a moment, the ancient hair will come back into view, and I'll resume that story.

The 5 percent of genes that matter, although a puny fragment, come in blizzard-size pieces. On average, a million base pairs contains only eleven genes. At this writing, the most-cited estimate is that the total number of human genes falls between twenty and twenty-five thousand, a disappointingly small number, and one likely to dwindle further. (It's fallen from a first estimate of one hundred thousand.) The human genome looks a lot like other mammal varieties, especially monkeys, and it's only about 5 percent bigger than *Rattus norvegicus*, the Norway rat, which is unwelcome news to most people. A species with a grasping and self-loving temperament wants a grander genome, an empire of genes, not a rat's portion.

SMALL, DIMINUTIVE, infinitesimal. The old adjectives don't convey the tiny-ness of molecular biology, or on the other end, the bigness of its numbers. As a result, writers have been humiliated, and the English language looks to the lab for size metaphors. Two prefixes have fallen into use from molecular computations—*nano* (Greek, "dwarf") and *giga*, for billion (Greek, "giant")—and more should be expected.

If nucleotides are so small and repetitive, how do they dictate traits, like aptitude for drawing, or combative behavior? Scientists and their acolytes in the press, science journalists, sometimes give simplistic answers when addressing the public. Molecular biologists, at least standing in front of a microphone, have been heard to deploy the "gene-for" explanation, claiming to find single genes that produce certain traits. The spin guarantees media coverage. (The hyperbole retreats six months later—it turns out there isn't a gay gene or an infidelity gene—but by that time, notice has been taken, and grants paid out for more study.) Due to overstatement, the idea has seized most people that there must be a one-to-one match between genes and traits. One result has been the takeover of medicine, as well as common sense, by a fresh form of determinism. People think they can possess genes for everything, from heart murmur to bad driving.

TERRY MELTON, the forensic specialist in hair, describes her lab protocol, what she plans to do with the sample in her lab at Mitotyping Technologies.

"We'll place the hair into a small tube with detergent that's good at removing proteinaceous material," she says. "Then it goes into an ultrasonic water bath for twenty minutes, three times, to vibrate off anything adhering to the outside. If you had epithelial cells, semen, sperm cells, blood cells—all those could be washed off. After that, the hairs are examined under a microscope for debris. Next, we grind it with a little glass grinder, like a mortar and pestle, which is used one time and thrown away. The ground hair is placed into a buffer solution that contains chemicals often found in beauty parlors. Dithiothreitol is one of them, which smells like perm solution. It breaks up the disulfide bonds in the hair, and that starts to break down the protein. The extraction process is essentially a way to purify the DNA away from everything else. At the end, you have a small tube of very pure, very clean DNA. From that you amplify with PCR—the polymerase chain reaction—the two hypervariable regions, which contain most of the variation that's found between individuals. You make lots of copies of those regions, then you sequence the DNA in those regions to know what the order of the chemical bases is, the nucleotides, those As, Ts, Cs, and Gs."

Melton slips easily into The Vocabulary. Molecular biology comes with layers of jargon, only a little of which has entered mass speech. DNA science differs in this way from the PC revolution, whose coinages seem always to bubble up from the technical underground into daily argot. One phrase of Melton's needs a gloss, because it is one of the keys to the old hair: the *hypervariable regions*.

A curious aspect of mitochondrial DNA is that, unlike the stringlike nuclear variety, DNA in mitochondria forms a circle. In 1981, researchers at Cambridge University sequenced the mitochondrial genome, transcribing the order of all the bases in this circular strand. Biologist Stephen Anderson gave each base a number, #1 to #16,569, and the outcome, called the Cambridge Reference Sequence, or sometimes, the

Anderson sequence, is the instrument for citing mitochondrial data. Hair examiners use the Cambridge sequence like a private language.

MtDNA, at 16,000 base pairs in length, is a mote next to its partner, nuDNA, with nearly three billion base pairs. In its brevity, mtDNA has been easier to study, and databases have bulked up with its sequence data. MtDNA contains genetic code to make thirteen proteins, and to do some other things, and it includes a short stretch of nucleotides that seem to do nothing. This bit of noncoding DNA numbers 1,123 nucleotides in length, a supremely tiny stretch of a molecule that's already trivial, and these 1,123 nucleotides go by the name of the "displacement loop." (The displacement loop peels away when the circular molecule duplicates itself, displacing the strand.) The order of nucleotides along this segment changes more often than other regions of the molecule. Two areas in particular change most often, a length 341 nucleotides long and another 267 nucleotides long. These little stretches, which together amount to one-thirtieth of the mtDNA genome, are the hypervariable regions. Hypervariable region 1 (HV1) runs from base 16,024 to 16,365 in the Cambridge Reference Sequence; HV2 encompasses bases 73 to 340.

When DNA replicates, during cell division, the copying process can make mistakes, resulting in mutations, a difference of a nucleotide here and there. With nuclear DNA, a proofreading mechanism compares the sequence for fidelity to the original and repairs the mutations before the cell is complete. In mitochondria, there's an apparent lack of DNA repair, and thus a higher rate of mutation. The hypervariable regions of mtDNA change at five or ten times the rate of nuDNA, with the result that in these sections of the genetic code, unrelated people, on average, possess one nucleotide of difference for each 100 nucleotides. The more such differences, the easier it is to catalog and chronicle genetic individuality.

The hypervariable regions provided one key to the old hair, because databases with hypervariable sequences had become common, and dense. If DNA could be pulled out of the hair, its sequences could be compared with racks of population data, and I could say something about the origins of this odd family group, who had cut their locks and stored them, like so much hidden genetic code.

3 *Out of Africa*

Isaac Ball was a princely businessman, dark-haired, severely handsome, and possibly vain. He and his wife, Eliza, started collecting hair during the 1820s. It wasn't eccentric, but a reaction to grief, after tragedy involving their children.

He owned several slave plantations, and evidence suggests that for much of his life Isaac was glib and materialistic. He'd been born in 1785, a third son, and he grew up in the soft grip of Southern gentry life. A glint of his vanity can be seen in a letter, written by Isaac's mother, that describes her boy, age thirteen, "his voice on the change," as flashing around the neighborhood in Charleston "in a squab duck coat—quite smart." As a child, Isaac was surrounded by enslaved servants and valets, men twice his age who brought him anything, ran the dogs when he hunted, opened the door as he approached. "He is brought up too much in the lap of indulgence," his mother wrote. "It's high time for him to shift a little for himself."

As a teenager, Isaac took up smoking, under the influence of his older brother, John. When he was twenty, he wrote his brother to say he'd quit tobacco, "and I shan't resume it until you lend a hand in corrupting me again." John Ball, shy and introverted, studious, was Isaac's temperamental opposite. Isaac liked possessions and style, disliked books. He declined to go to college, enrolling in a kind of finishing school for boys run by a Dr. George Buist, a course that smoothed his manners. As a reward for this mediocre achievement, when Isaac turned twenty-one, his father gave him a phaeton, an expensive, lacquered, four-seat carriage that was the limousine of its day. Isaac cruised in the coach, driven by a black driver dressed in livery, riding around Charleston, preening.

The phaeton was supposed to help him find adulthood, as well as a wife, but it did neither. A letter from a relative who'd heard of the carriage expressed hope: "Isaac being now set up in style . . . he may make an attack on Miss Conny, and in the course of a few months I hope to hear of his being fast bound in the Hymeneal knot." But Miss Conny rejected him, and a year later, another woman to whom Isaac proposed also turned him down.

In 1809, Isaac retreated to the resort of Newport, Rhode Island, to nurse the wounds to his ego. He advertised self-pity in a letter to John: "Tomorrow's sun ushers me into my

25th year . . . [leaving me] a solitary bachelor. I feel horrid & if it were not sinful would curse the day that gave birth to so useless a creature. . . . Still, I shall endeavor to drink you many happy returns of the day . . . with a bumper of Adams Ale."

Isaac's aimlessness came to an end when an uncle died, leaving him two plantations and two villages of enslaved workers. "I give to my nephew Isaac Ball my Plantation known by the Name of Limerick, whereon I now reside," said the uncle's will, "and also a Plantation called the Cypress." The uncle, Elias Ball III, the fat and gout-suffering bachelor slaveholder, would also bequeath Isaac the secretary, later hiding place of the hair collection. The desk awaited Isaac at Limerick plantation when he moved there, in 1810.

Flaunting two profitable estates, Isaac was finally able to persuade a woman to marry him. Eliza Catherine Poyas was twenty-five, mild and pious, oval-faced and sad-eyed, with light hair parted in the middle. A physician's daughter, she came from a plantation a few miles up the road. Isaac and Eliza had known each other all their lives, and they'd played together as children. They were second cousins; their grandmothers had been sisters. Eliza's parents were well-off, which was the main thing, and so their marriage at the relatively advanced age of their mid-twenties was met with relief.

Whereas Isaac's brother, John, lived in a comparatively modest house, Isaac's appetite for display was overwhelming. In 1815, he bought an acre in Charleston and hired contractors to build a mansion. Two years later, Isaac and

Eliza possessed a three-story house the size of a hotel, with parlors like auditoriums, rivers of woodwork in the Federal style, stables, gardens, and a separate tenement in the back for the twenty or so domestic slaves assigned to maintain everything. Construction receipts report that the house had required 199,850 bricks.

Isaac and Eliza now had two houses, the city mansion and the Limerick house, twenty-five miles north of town. Style was central: Isaac followed English fashion, subscribing to the *European*, a quarterly guide to taste sent from London. He and Eliza sat for their portraits and hung them in the ballroom. The painting of Isaac shows him at about age thirty-five, dressed in an unstructured Empire jacket and collarless white shirt, his hair combed forward in the Napoleonic style. It was the decade of Waterloo.

The couple tried for children, but after seven years of marriage, none had appeared. The expected thing was that such a couple, passengers in what Eliza's Aunt Betsy would call "society," would have had four or five children. Eliza and Isaac wanted some semblance of a family, and in 1818 Eliza persuaded a brother of hers to let the two of them raise one of his sons. A five-year-old boy named James was moved to Limerick, perhaps bewildered, to play the part of son.

As sometimes happens with an adoption, Eliza then got pregnant. Two years later, she was pregnant again. She had four children in five years: Isaac (in 1818), Eliza (1820), William (1821), and Jane (1823). Longing for a partner, lengthy disappointment, adoption, and a sustained blast of fertility, the catharsis of all that had gone before. All seemed well, the houses were finally full. The plantations minted money, and Isaac bought more of them. His family took its place among the privileged.

The secretary, in late 1824, stood in the main house at Limerick plantation. It served as Isaac's office, and perhaps as the writing table of his wife. It was Christmastime, and Eliza was once again pregnant, though just a month along. She and her husband chose this moment to begin snipping hair from family members.

Before photography, the only pictures of people were paintings made by portrait artists. Cost, as well as perhaps bad artists, made them scarce. It may have been that Eliza and Isaac wanted mementos, visual keepsakes of the people around them; hence the hair, which was plentiful and personal. But in this instance, the decision to collect family hair must have been anything but casual.

In February 1824, the couple's first daughter, four-year-old Eliza, died, probably from malaria. A few months later, Isaac wrote one of his relatives with news of a second death, that of his oldest son, from yellow fever. "A total of 236 persons [in Charleston] have died," Isaac said, "and among the number it has pleased the Almighty to take my son Isaac who died on the 11th of October after an illness of 21 days." The boy was six. Between the first death and the second, only nine months.

The funerals changed Isaac. The language of his letters deflates; his meticulous business records went neglected. *(If our children die, what will we remember of them?)* And so around Christmas, 1824—maybe Christmas week, with its sentimental grip—the parents cut a lock of hair from their

remaining natural son, William Ball, age three. William wouldn't have understood why he had to give up a finger-length of his curls. But for his parents, the lock of hair felt like insurance against losing their children.

Other family members, some of them adults, soon contributed snippets. Isaac's brother, John, forty-two now, gave his part. John Ball's sample appears in a folded piece of the heavy paper he preferred for his stationery, with his signature on it. After John, a cousin added some hair, and another cousin, and the collection grew.

If Isaac and Eliza were arming themselves against the forgetfulness of death, it was no use, because a year after the first hair had been stored, Isaac Ball contracted malaria and died, at age forty. His youngest child, John, was three months old.

The hair collecting stopped. Eliza, Isaac's widow, mustn't have had the stomach for it. After losing two children and her husband in a span of eighteen months, she saw hair mementos as frivolous.

Eliza Ball was left with four young children and a plantation empire. Her photographs from later years give a glimpse of her wounds. In them, her face is long and remote, and she always wears black. Eliza lived forty-two years after her husband's death, and she never remarried. Dutifully, she stayed at Limerick plantation during the winter—it had been her husband's, and the place to which she'd come as a bride. But in summer and fall, Eliza always fled the place, moving to the city or to a house near the ocean. These were the months of fever, and fever was the cull that had taken all of them.

THE FETISH OF LABELED and dated hair, odd as it may appear, seems to have been normal for the period. When Isaac Ball died, in 1825, a relative in England wrote his widow with a condolence gift that consisted of a pin with hair: "I sent out a small packet in April [1826] to you containing a . . . brooch with my husband Austin's hair and my own," this cousin said (in a letter housed in the library at Duke University).

In the mid-1800s, a magazine out of Philadelphia called *Godey's Lady's Book* packaged poetry and decorating ideas for middle-class subscribers. The May 1855 issue found the editors giving approval to jewelry made from the hair of one's dead children. "Hair is at once the most delicate and lasting of our materials, and it survives us like love," said the unsigned comment. "With a lock of hair belonging to a child, we may almost look up to heaven and compare notes with angelic nature, may almost say, 'I have a piece of thee here.'"

The Henry Ford Museum opened in 1929 near Detroit to house Mr. Ford's collection of Americana—clothing, ads, toys, machines, cookware, furniture. In building his warehouse of everyday life, as he saw it, his collection for the public good, Mr. Ford asked an architect to make a copy of Philadelphia's Independence Hall and to place it at an emblematic site, near the grinding, belching Ford River Rouge plant, itself a mile-long blast of American-ness.

Passing through the rooms of plows and steam engines, penny whistles and office furniture, the visitor to the museum comes to a collection of brooches and bracelets made with locks of human hair. In a sea of wholesome mechanisms, it is a stomach-twittering display. The heavy gold brooch with red gemstones has a compartment for strands of hair around the back. The "Woven Hair Bracelet with Pendant" (dated 1856) is a braided length that attaches to the wrist.

Jewelry made from hair was popular for much of the nineteenth century, but the Ford Museum is one of only two or three collections in the country that possess hair jewelry. Why so rare? Is the absence of hair jewelry from design collections due to its morbid pall, because it is one ornament that brings you close to death?

The fad for hair mementos started in the Empire period and became a mass phenomenon by mid-century. Prosperous women, confined to the house, made handcrafts with strands of hair, winding tresses into earrings and necklaces, sitting in groups to talk and weave in a kind of hirsute quilting bee. Hair ornaments matured with "mourning jewelry" during and after the Civil War. The war killed more than 600,000, and jewelers responded with prefabricated hair lockets, coin-sized glass cases in which hair from a dead son or husband could be stored, often twisted into a flower shape. The locket would hang from a necklace or, on fathers of dead soldiers, from a watch fob. Memorial rings made entirely from woven hair released the strongest emotions, because they put the deceased's hair in contact with the skin of the finger.

A twenty-first-century feeling of superior taste might declare hair jewelry to be kitsch or repellent. Among buyers of antique jewelry, no one much likes Victorian hair lockets, which fall near the bottom of the price spread at flea markets. Their gothic aspect is unmistakable. Not only might hair jewelry contain the hair of a dead person, the woman who first owned the thing is also dead.

The nineteenth-century obsession with hair seems to have climaxed with the Seven Sutherland Sisters of Lockport, New York. The Sutherland women, musicians and performers (piano, voice, violin), were said to have collective head hair totaling thirty-seven feet (postcards of the sisters show them at a three-quarter angle to the camera, their hair swept in front of their shoulders, draped to the floor). After years of performing in the Northeast, the women joined the Barnum and Bailey Circus. By this time, their father, a Methodist minister named Fletcher Sutherland, noticed that audiences paid more attention to his daughters' hair than to their music. He devised a mysterious bottled

The Seven Sutherland Sisters, about 1890.

sauce, the Seven Sutherland Sisters Hair Grower, profits from which allowed the women to retire from the circus and lifted their many dependents into posh townhouses for a generation or two. The Sutherland Sisters make the ancient hair look less strange as an artifact.

Only three months old when his father died, John Ball seems to have been chosen by his mother, Eliza, to be her companion in widowhood. They couldn't be separated during his childhood, and when Eliza Ball decided to vacation in England, in 1845, she chose John, then nineteen years old, to go with her. Eliza kept a diary on the trip, and its pages place the two in memorable circumstances. One day, when they were at Ramsgate, the seaside resort in Kent, Eliza and John went out to watch the swimmers. "Crowds go daily to the sands," Eliza wrote, "where bathing cars are kept for their accommodation, and are drawn by a horse into the water." In the 1840s, people who rode carriages into the ocean were clothed, neck to ankle.

A revealing incident took place a bit later, in London. Eliza had brought John to the city for what she felt was an important appointment. It seems she was keen to trace the family's ancestry, and this was the place to do it, with her son and heir. Several people back home had assured her that aristocratic blood ran somewhere in the family's origins. The appointment of the day, the rendezvous that might prove it, brought Eliza to a place called the College of Arms, the royal repository for coats of arms and pedigrees of British families. In short, a registry concerned with un-American things like titles and royal honors, and with an accounting of who possessed what symbol. The College ruled on which families actually had earned a coat of arms and thus who should be permitted to claim one. Then, as now, the College of Arms stood in Queen Victoria Street. On the appointed day, Eliza hired a hackney cab, and, with hopes of impressing both herself and her son, headed to the seventeenth-century building behind St. Paul's Cathedral. "John and I went to the Herald's office to search for the Coat of Arms of our family," Eliza wrote, "and the officer could not find it from the information we could give, so paid five shillings fee for nothing, and three shillings for the cab."

Eliza had been frustrated that she couldn't find the thing

to which she'd felt entitled—a title. It's a funny spectacle, a would-be aristocrat who complains about cab fare, but Eliza stands for something in the people who'd collected the hair. Many in the family of Isaac and Eliza regarded themselves as part of an old, elite line stretching to the medieval past and beyond. The clerk at the College of Arms had called their bluff.

A later generation might say that Eliza had been looking for her genetic origins. Would the DNA from the hair help? Would it be possible to trace a line to the place where some of the family genes actually originated?

One can say anything about the deceased, who have no right to privacy. Libel law doesn't apply to the dead, because they have no legal standing: they can't sue. But it didn't seem fair to scrutinize the poor, defenseless hair specimens, perhaps exposing the secrets of their owners, without taking personal risk. In a break from forensic protocol, I decided to test my own DNA while awaiting results on the hair.

DNA arrives at a lab in different vehicles, blood and saliva being the most common. A typical carrier is a buccal swab (pronounced *buckle*), a cell collection made by scraping a cotton-tipped stick on the inside cheek. I found a company in North Carolina called Tritech USA that supplied buccal swab kits to law enforcement agencies. A call to the office, and a baritone voice came on the line, projecting authority.

"This is Tritech. We wrote the book on buccal swab collection kits. Not bragging." Baritone Voice listened to my request for swab kits, then asked probative questions. "Who are you?" was one of them. "What, exactly, will the test be used for?" another. The answers didn't impress, and Baritone Voice turned suspicious. "I'm sorry, I'm going to back out of this one. We do not sell swab kits to civilians. Don't take offense, but we don't want these things to get into the wrong hands." And *blick*, he was gone.

Buccal swab kits consist of two seven-inch sticks, which look like long Q-tips, plus an envelope in which to mail them. They don't give the impression of contraband. But we live in manufactured fear. The encounter with Baritone Voice had provided a lesson: DNA science buzzes with anxiety, a tension perhaps derived from its magic.

One company, DNAPrint Genomics, had cleverly joined "DNA" to "fingerprint" to create its name (and sent out swab kits, no questions). Their specialty was analysis of ancestry. I chose the company's "biogeographical ancestry test." DNAPrint had created the protocol, which was a piece of intellectual property. The test compared one's sequence data to genetic databases and inferred things about one's family history. Research behind the test had come from an academic, an anthropologist at Pennsylvania State University named Mark Shriver. Shriver had shown that by looking at 170 or more sites in the test-taker's DNA, one could infer the geographic origins of that individual's ancestors, whether they (or some of them) had lived in Asia, Europe, Africa, or North America.

The test investigated something called admixture. Shriver argues that Americans possess a lot of unacknowledged admixture, the blending of genes from several places. White people may look "European," and black people "African," but for 500 years much of the world has sent migrants to the Americas. In the Western Hemisphere, Africans and Europeans, and Asians and Native Americans, have all mixed. As a result, American whites possess genes from all around the world, as do Latinos, Native Americans, and blacks. The company's test makes an estimate of the admixture, the ratio of the mix in the individual who sends in a buccal swab.

The collection kit arrived, a pair of sticks with soft, ribbed ends. A quick scrub to collect cells, and the sticks went into an envelope, with a consent form and check, back to the company.

When the database known as CODIS went into operation, one of the initial sorting devices designed by the FBI was one for race identity. Police wanted to run a DNA sequence taken from trace evidence and return, if not a match, then at least the supposed ethnicity of a suspect. DNAPrint, the lab to which I'd sent the buccal swab, was in a similar business. It used genetic markers for what it called "the four major historical population groups . . . Sub-Saharan African, Indo-European, East Asian, and Native American." When DNAPrint analyzed a swab, the company returned a report that estimated percentage amounts for the genetic contribution to the sample of each population group.

Suppose that a Chinese-American woman, born in the United States, has three grandparents who emigrated from China fifty years ago, and one grandparent who is a white

American. Read in a certain way, the DNA sequence in the woman's saliva would be sufficient to identify her as being "one-quarter Indo-European" and "three-quarters East Asian." This kind of molecular certainty is interesting, but also creepy. Interesting, because it is done without reference to a photograph or interview; creepy, because it sounds like the race formulas of the Jim Crow period, when the Census Bureau used categories like "one-quarter Negro."

The analysis depends on a story of human origins that came out of DNA labs. It's a science from the late 1980s, and it has a movie-title name, the "out-of-Africa model."

In 1987, the journal *Nature* published a five-page paper, "Mitochondrial DNA and Human Evolution," by Allan Wilson, a New Zealand–born geneticist at the University of California, Berkeley, and two of his graduate students. Wilson's group had examined DNA samples from 147 volunteers whose families had originated on five different continents. The paper looked at variations in the mitochondrial DNA of each, and these differences allowed Wilson to sort the samples into clusters; the clusters, in turn, happened to correspond to the self-reported geographic origins of the volunteers.

The genetic patterns that characterized Wilson's volunteers reflected population movements dating back tens of thousands of years. For instance, the mtDNA of Native Americans possessed certain variations, a subset of which was shared with East Asians, as though the two had once been the same population, but had diverged. In a similar way, the sequences of people from northern India overlapped with those of Europeans, as though they'd also been a single population, but had split apart. The paper showed how DNA differences could be interpreted to form a chronicle of these changes—a story of populations shaping and dividing, again and again—and to create something called a phylogenetic tree that traced the evolution and movement of human groups over vast lengths of time. Wilson's analysis supported the theory that anatomically modern humans had originated in Africa, then had migrated out and around the world—the out-of-Africa model.

Allan Wilson's lab established evolutionary genetics, a field that uses DNA to talk about what happened in deep history, long before written records, in time frames where archaeological evidence is thin. His achievement (Wilson died in 1991) was to show how DNA could be used to create a kind of global family tree, with branches and lines of descent, all of which lead back to Africa. Looking at diversity and mutation rates of DNA in living people, Wilson and his protégés devised species development maps (phylogenetic trees, which look like crowded ancestry charts). The trees imply the appearance of a single small group of common human ancestors, perhaps 10,000 people, probably in central Africa, and the branching of all humanity from it into the current range of populations and body types. Out-of-Africa is the name for this evolutionary script.

The out-of-Africa story, in capsule form, is this: Perhaps 200,000 years ago, anatomically modern humans arose in Africa, and in time, this population swelled and covered the continent. About 100,000 years ago (give or take, because the dates fluctuate, depending on the math that calculates mutation rates), a small subset of people in East Africa left the continent via the Sinai Peninsula. All populations outside of those in Africa descend from this initial group of migrants. From the Middle East, the outlanders split, one group spreading east and south along the Indian Ocean, the other, west and north into Europe. (Papers published after Allan Wilson's death shorten the time line and estimate that migrants crossed into the Middle East more recently.) The movement was gradual, less than a mile per generation; but en route, modern humans displaced or overwhelmed humanlike others, such as Neanderthals, until the migration wrapped the world.

Before out-of-Africa, much archaeology had assumed a different account of human development, the so-called multiregional hypothesis. Multiregionalism claimed humans arose on several continents at the same time, from similar apelike predecessors, and that these branches blended into a single world population. According to out-of-Africa, the archaic species of humans (*Homo erectus, Australopithecus*) don't really form a part of modern human ancestry. These branches were not-quite-people, and they died out. Modern humans (*Homo sapiens*) might have encountered such other species on the slow trek around the world (for example, Neanderthals in Europe), but humans didn't mate with them: they replaced them.

Time lines loosen when you write history with genes, since DNA-time comes in 10,000-year blocks. The 500-year Euro-American expansion flattens to a wafer, and the three-age system of archaeological dating looks pretty brief, too (the Bronze Age, 3000–1000 before the Christian era; the Neolithic, 10,000–3000 BCE; and the Paleolithic, prior to 10,000 BCE). Rather than dating evidence by, say, carbon decay, DNA dating uses genetic markers as historical units of time.

A marker is a site on a chromosome that's used as a sign or reference point to map genetic events. (Go down to this big gene and turn left.) The use of markers to date human happenings works by correlating mutations with historical events. If the population of Alphaland possesses a certain DNA profile, and the population of Betaland the same profile, plus one variation, that variation is said to be a marker, and it can be inferred that Betaland broke off from Alphaland some thousands of years ago. If Betaland possesses two variations, the two groups are likely to have diverged twice as far in the past. The out-of-Africa model, with its chronicle based on genetic variation, is a gift of DNA science to history that gives the means to narrate human events over a very long period.

DNAPrint, the testing company, used the out-of-Africa model, in conjunction with markers that have accumulated in particular regions of the world, as two instruments to say something about individual ancestry. A marker proven to have appeared in Europe in the last 10,000 years means that the person who carries it must have had, at some point, European family members. An example of a non-European marker is the FY*0 variation, in the so-called Duffy locus. The FY*0 variation is a nearly universal variant in black (sub-Saharan) Africa, but it's entirely missing in Europe. It appears in the Duffy locus, a segment of chromosome 1 that contains genes that code for a protein found on the surface of red blood cells. FY*0, also known as the Duffy-null variation, is an adaptation that provides some immunity to malaria, the parasite disease that affects red blood cells. One source of malaria, which must enter the red cells to live, is *Plasmodium vivax*, and *vivax* malaria requires an enabler, a kind of biological travel agent, known as the Duffy protein. Without the Duffy protein on the red cell surface, *vivax* can't enter the cell. FY*0 signals a genetic failure to produce the Duffy protein. Because the variation appears throughout sub-Saharan Africa, a person with the marker FY*0 is certain to have had black African ancestry, in addition to a good chance of surviving malaria.

My family is white and always has been. Both of my parents came from people in the South who, for generations, have paid close attention to their European roots. A case could be made that some of us in the family, perhaps Eliza Ball, have at times been mesmerized by our so-called pedigree (a word once used without irony in the South). Our whiteness is a subject so settled that to question it is preposterous, like a father asking his son if he's a boy. Thus, to send a cheek swab for an ethnicity test was a bit of a ruse; the results were certain to show our European origins.

The buccal swab had gone out to DNAPrint, and a CD-ROM came back with a report. Some pages of discussion, in business-ese ("We're pleased to enclose . . ."), plus raw data, in lab-speak:

Number 1113 rs1800498

TACTGTCTGCATTCTAAGATATAAGCATCAAGTGTTTGGAACAGTGCCT
GACACATGGTAAGTCCTTAGTATTATTACAGTTATTAGGACTTAGCTGAG

CCAGCTCAGGGCCTGTACTGCAGGTCTCAGCTTTATGTGAGCAAGAGC
ATTAAGGAATGATGCCTGGATGCCTGGGGGTGTGAAGAAAAGAGCCTT
GGGTT [C/T] GACTAGGGAACCTGGGGCCACTCCTTCCTCTGCTACTAA
ATCACCAAGTGATCTTGTTCTGTTTTCTTCTCTGACCCTCCCTAGTTTT
GTCCACCCTTGAAATAATCATCTTTCCTTTTCACATTTCATGCTTACCAA
GTACTTGTCACCTAATTATCTCCTCTCTTGATAAGCTAGATGGTYCCTTC
CAGGGCAGCTTA

Number 1116 rs3340

GGTGGAGAGCACTTAAAAACAAAATGAATGATCAATATGAGGGGCCAA
AGTCCTTCATTCTTTTTCAAAACATTCCTCAAAACCTTTTTTTTTTTTTT
TTTGGTGAAAACCACTTAGAAATCGAATACGTCCATTTCTTTGTAAAAT
AACAATAACGTT [G/A] AAGGCAAAAGCAAGATTCTGTAAACCAACATT
GGAAAAGGGGACACAGGGAGGGGCAGAGGGAAAGGGCCAGATTTTCA
ACGGTTTCCTCCACATCTGCAGACAAAGGCCCGCCTACTCT

And so on. The alternation in the report between plain English and gibberish looked unstable, like a mental patient who drifts from sense into echolalia and back. Here was the secret dialect of DNA. The data were straightforward, but it looked as though something lay hidden inside.

A bit of reading around, and the code gave way. Each paragraph of unbroken capitals ("TACTGTC . . .") referred to a different marker or segment of the DNA molecule. The first marker (number 1,113) ran to 402 nucleotides in length, with each nucleotide represented by a capital letter. Within the markers were tiny, significant bits of information called "single nucleotide polymorphisms," or SNPs. (The acronym is preferred, and it's pronounced *snip*.) A SNP is a difference, between the DNA of two individuals, of one link in the nucleotide chain (single nucleotide polymorphism = a one link variation).

SNPs are like freckles on DNA. They are the smallest, finest grain of genetic difference. Millions of SNPs have been cataloged, and they generally don't affect the body's functions. But (back to out-of-Africa) if you compare SNPs across the continents, they become signs that let you infer something about a person's ancestry. People from West Africa have some SNPs, which have appeared over thousands of years, and those from China, others.

On the DNAPrint report, "Number 1113" was the number for one of the 170 markers the lab had chosen to test. And "rs1800498" meant reference SNP 1800498, a number assigned by the National Center for Biotechnology Information, a corner of the U.S. Department of Health and Human Services that keeps a database of the millions of SNPs.

A chart interpreted the indigestible data, giving percentages for the population contributions within the DNA sample. The page labeled "Maximum Likelihood Estimate" (statistical slang for "our best guess") contained the kernel of information that mattered. Which was this: the test suggested that about 13 percent of my genes were Native American.

I paused and looked. Indian? If this were true, much of the family history—the European roots, the white genealogy—would have to be reimagined.

Science, the secular religion. People believe things when a scientist utters them. I dislike the field's grandeur and its supposed monopoly on truth. But could there be something to these results? Isn't DNA the master code, the hard drive of biological memory?

"Thirteen percent Native American" meant about one in eight. Two parents, four grandparents, eight great-grandparents; in theory, it was consistent with one of my great-grandparents having been an Indian. No way.

I thought about my Native American "experience." I'd visited a couple of archaeological sites in the Southwest, but never an Indian reservation. I'd met Native Americans, but I no longer had their phone numbers. Indian ancestry? No one on either side of the family had said a word.

4 Americanus rubescus

William Ball ("WJ Ball's hair—aged 3 years 1824") was the third child of Isaac and Eliza. His father had died in 1825, when William turned four, and the boy had inherited his parents' place, Limerick plantation. William's mother shuttled her children between the family's two houses, raising them alone, but in reality she wasn't a single mother, because enslaved women did most of the work. Accountants would manage William's property for the next seventeen years, until his twenty-first birthday, a day that, in Willaim's view, didn't come quickly enough.

As a boy, William seems to have been a melancholy prince. His wants were always answered, and he did much what he liked, but there is no record of pranks or fun, as there is with some of his cousins. Well-behaved, conservatively dressed, he affected a businesslike mien.

Although he was a poor student, at seventeen William obediently left home for South Carolina College, in nearby Columbia. Some of his letters from school survive, and they give a glimpse of his mind. He wanted his inheritance and was tired of the wait. "I didn't mean to say that a college education was useless," he told his mother in one letter. "I meant to say that I thought it of not much importance to me. The English would laugh at us if they could see exactly how little we did here, and then call it a college education."

Despite playing at being an adult, William didn't possess a stoical temperament. From school, he complained, "We get nothing to eat. . . . I think that even the servants at home fare far better than I do and consequently, I always come back to my room sorrowing." William consoled himself with music. He studied guitar with a German instructor; later, his own children would be among the most musically adept in the family.

At age twenty, William dropped out of college and came home. He was handsome but gangly. Later photographs show a wiry and uncomfortable figure in jackets, and his hair looked bristly and dark, a change from the soft lock his parents had saved. The overdue twenty-first birthday was imminent, so William proposed to one of his cousins, a fragile seventeen-year-old named Julia Cart. She was more petite than William's mother, but she looked a bit like her, with sad eyes and hair pulled back. Julia moved into the big house at Limerick plantation, joining her new husband and her mother-in-law. The design of the house, with bedrooms on the second floor all facing a central hall and stairs, meant that William's mother probably slept across the hall from the master bedroom, perhaps to the discouragement of the young wife.

Despite this obstacle, Julia became pregnant right away. After the delivery, or perhaps after the next child, William and Julia decided to renew the family tradition that William's parents had started and that his mother had sensibly abandoned. A thick blond lock from Isaac Ball, born to Julia in 1844 and named for his grandfather, is the first from this second phase of haircuts. Next is a specimen from "Aunt Cingie," William's great-aunt on his father's side. Another lock, "Aunt Betsy's hair," came from Elizabeth Poyas, the writer. Probably the two aunts had come for a visit together, and the talk turned to "the hair thing your mother used to do." William's mother was in the house, and may have pointed to the scissors. A couple of cousins also contributed hair, and an in-law; and so it went again, the collection growing when one or another relative would take an interest in it and add something.

Julia Ball had four sons: William, Isaac, John, and Elias. Their parents waited, then grabbed a bit of their hair and stored it. (Locks from two of the boys are missing, which may mean that their hair ended up with them, or their own children.) The family group grew to seven—William, his mother, his wife, and children. Since they hadn't moved, and since the furniture had remained, with additions, for fifty years, the old desk sat in the same place, or near it, and the hair probably went piece by piece into its safe pocket.

But in the 1850s, the hair collecting stopped. It seems

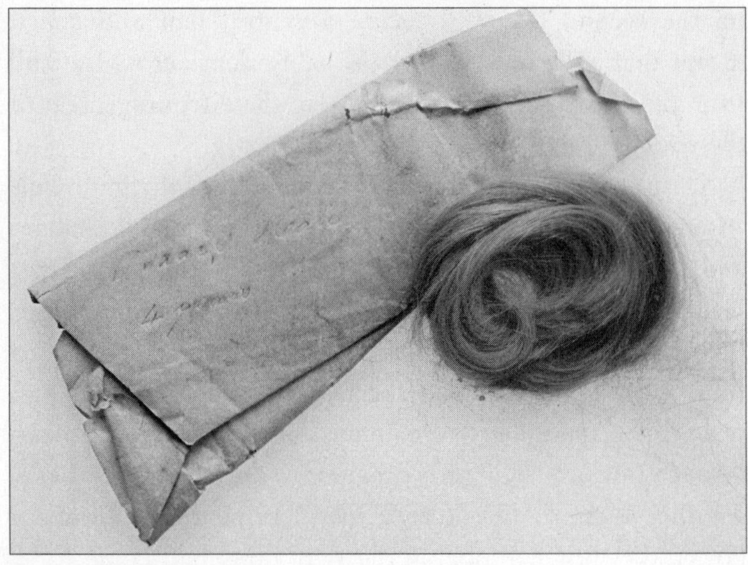

there was no tragedy on this occasion, but something else had happened to make the preoccupation moot. A photographer had come to Charleston, a daguerreotype artist, to be precise, possibly a man touring the South with his newfangled camera apparatus. Daguerreotypes captured people's faces on a little silver plate, and these pictures challenged the need for hair mementos, because it was possible to have images of one's children and not just their forelocks. About 1855, William had some ten daguerreotypes made, one each of most family members. The last lock of hair dates from this time, and I doubt it was coincidence. The hair collecting ended, obsolete, and never started up again.

Julia Ball's daguerrotype shows a handsome but weak woman, and tradition says that although she'd birthed four sons, she was "sickly." In 1858, after years of illness, Julia died, at age thirty-four, in the summer. William waited four years, then he remarried, with little more than a week's notice, during the middle of the Civil War. His second wife was a woman named Mary Gibbs, his first cousin, who lived at a plantation three miles away. The haste of it surprised, and because William's four sons were away from home, in Confederate units, they couldn't attend. This was probably in William's plan: he might not have wanted his boys to see their forty-two-year-old father choose a twenty-six-year-old replacement for their mother.

This time William had misjudged, in that the neighbors regarded the marriage as a mistake, and William and Mary went down poorly as a couple. In a letter to his mother, the bridegroom complained that nobody visited, and friends didn't ask about his wife. The age difference may not have mattered—widowed men often reached down for young wives—but wartime fussiness did. "She should marry a soldier, after it's over," might have been the view.

In fact, there had been a bigger gaffe. For some time, William's oldest son, Willie, had been engaged to his new stepmother's younger sister, Maria. Willie was in the war, and couldn't marry, and it's likely that he didn't appreciate his father bride-shopping at the same address where he'd gone to the trouble of finding a fiancée before shouldering a gun to defend the Southern way of life. Family lore has it that when William (the father) got engaged, he asked Willie (the son) to break off his engagement. Willie refused. After the surrender, he came home and married as planned, with the result that father and son had married sisters. It was Willie who had to move out.

Late in William's life, dislocation marked everything. His four sons survived the war and arrived home, demoralized. His slaves had been freed, and most of them had left. The old class system was coming apart, and William couldn't adjust. To pay debts, he sold his plantations, except for the one where he lived, Limerick. He'd been an heir at age four and a rich businessman until his mid-forties. The last quarter-century of his life felt like a long decline, as life went from soft, to a little less soft. In his sixties, William regarded himself as poor and straitened, and his family as having been abused by fate. But he was glad that some things had stayed the same. Writing in a diary, twenty-five years after the Civil War, he confided (to himself, one assumes) that he still employed some of his former slaves. "We still have two of our old servants with us," he wrote. "Thank God they have never left us."

THE "INDIAN" CONTRIBUTION to my DNA had put a crack in the windshield; or perhaps it had broken the rear-view mirror, since after all it was about genes and about the past. It would have to be corroborated with other tests, which, with any luck, would include tests on the hair. William Ball's hair was the oldest sample and the one closest to the colonial years, when Native Americans and whites had lived side by side. I took the hair to California.

A lab near San Francisco, Trace Genetics, specialized in DNA markers associated with Indian ancestry. The company consisted of two recent PhDs in genetics, plus a small staff. Jason Eshleman and Ripan Malhi, while they were graduate students, had worked on the remains of Kennewick Man, a skeleton found beside the Columbia River near Kennewick, Washington, and said to be that of a man who'd lived 9,000 years ago. Kennewick Man might have been Native American, or he might not have been—the argument between anthropologists continued—but the case had done much to prep the two geneticists for the old hair.

Trace Genetics occupied a few rooms in an office park north of Berkeley. Ripan Malhi was the son of Indian parents—from Asia, the India that Columbus had failed to encounter—who'd emigrated from Punjab to America. He pronounced his name *Rippin',* and he looked to be about thirty. He wore a brown leather bomber jacket, red-and-black striped shirt, and worn blue jeans. An orblike pendant on a leather string hung from his neck. He was about five-feet nine, with dark hair, a full face, and black, wire-rimmed glasses.

Malhi's customers are mostly people of European ancestry who believe from family legend that they have some kind of Native American connection. "They seem to have a similar story," Malhi says. "There is some lore about Native ancestry, which their grandmother never talked about, probably because they would have been discriminated against. And now they want to know."

The company's main asset is its database, comprising several thousand DNA sequences of Native Americans, "geographically spread out, linguistically mixed." By comparing a sequence from a new sample to sequences in the database, Malhi gains an idea whether the customers in question possessed any "Indian" markers.

Malhi says that not all clients come for cultural or sentimental reasons: some want money. There had been press in California about members of Indian tribes receiving money simply for belonging to a community. Some customers wanted genetic tests to help them enroll in such a tribe. As it happens, most tribes don't use DNA to determine membership, but other things, including documents and genealogies, which add up to something called "blood quantum."

Blood quantum is a definition of identity left over from legal segregation. In the United States until about 1965, and in South Africa until 1994, apartheid laws referred to the "quantity of blood" that an individual might carry from a given race. Native American tribes and the Interior Department, which oversees Indian politics, still use the concept.

I gave a bit of William Ball's hair to Trace Genetics, as well as hair from Isaac Ball, one of his sons. William had collected a blond lock of hair from four-year-old Isaac in 1848. If either sample possessed "Indian" markers, it would give credibility to my alleged 13-percent Native American blood quantum.

TO JUDGE FROM their taste in poetry, William Ball and family had been deaf to literature. Nowhere does anyone refer to Wordsworth or Whitman, but with some regularity in their papers and letters, family members jotted down ditties and rhymes. Chunks of bad verse appear in notes between relatives during this period, with many simply copied from pamphlets or songs. One verse that somebody saved suggests how William's family might have felt about Indians.

It's an anonymous stanza, and it seems to have come from the first owner of the old desk, Elias Ball III, who'd written it down sometime after the Revolutionary War. I found the verse among family files in a historical society in Charleston, copied on a many-holed, yellowed piece of paper, dating from about 1790, shuffled in with some other miscellany.

I'll tell you my friends a most comical joke,
How I learned all the squaws and the Indians to
smoke.
For in less than one month by the sun & the stars,
They smoked seven thousand three hundred cigars.
And then to be sure, as you'd naturally think,
After learning to smoke, they were all made to
drink.
I taught them to walk, too, as straight as a line,
After drinking four hundred good gallons of wine.
The next thing I taught them pray hear me repeat,
After drinking and smoking I learned them to eat.
But the worst of it all is the story that follows
It cost our great nation fifty thousand dollars.
At length by such smoking and drinking and eating,
All the squaws and papooses were given a beating.
And then I prescribed what you know is the dandy,
First bitters, then cordials, then porter and brandy.

Most Indians had been driven out of South Carolina by 1800. The people who saved the hair probably didn't know any Indians, but their grandparents, the generation of Elias

Ball III, had indeed had dealings with Native people. At that time, many tribes lived along the rivers in South Carolina, where whites alternately did business with and went to war against them. As the fitful and nasty verse suggests, Indians were looked on as playthings, marionettes to be pulled around a bit before being tossed back onto the pile of toys.

THE TERM "ANCIENT DNA" refers to a genetic sample older than a few years. Bones of mummies qualify, as did the hair samples. The first ancient DNA extraction occurred in China in 1982, with results published, as one might expect, in Mandarin. Few non-Chinese biologists read the paper, and gossip went around that the experimental standards hadn't been ideal. Thus, outside China, the field of ancient DNA is said to have started up in 1984, when Russell Higuchi, a researcher at the University of California, Berkeley, was able to extract DNA from a preserved bit of an extinct animal. The mammal had possessed a melodic name—the quagga.

Russell Higuchi, middle aged, mild, dressed in khakis and green polo shirt, sits at his desk in an eight-by-ten-foot office at Roche Diagnostics, the giant Swiss-owned drug company, where he's worked for much of his adult life. His office lies a half-hour south of Berkeley. At Roche, Higuchi has devised improvements in DNA analysis, including one applied in most labs. He's well known and highly praised. The quagga thing was something he did as a younger man, a stunt.

Higuchi has an introverted, sweet manner and likes a self-deprecating joke. In that vein, he's brought out an old copy of the *National Enquirer,* which contains an article that refers to him. "Dinosaurs Being Cloned for Defense," the headline states. When, in 1984, Higuchi published his ancient DNA piece in *Nature* magazine ("DNA sequences from the quagga, an extinct member of the horse family"), a media rush ensued, and the *National Enquirer* picked up the story. The *Enquirer* piece depicted Higuchi as a crazed scientist with the ethics of Dr. Frankenstein.

Allan Wilson, of the out-of-Africa model, was lab director at Berkeley in the 1980s, and Russell Higuchi was one of his students. "Wilson collected old things, museum specimens, like a piece of a woolly mammoth carcass, frozen in Siberia," Higuchi says. It was through Wilson that Higuchi got interested in the quagga.

When white settlers came from northern Europe to southern Africa during the eighteenth century to set up colonial outposts, they encountered millions of quaggas. The animals looked like zebras, except their stripes gradually vanished toward the hindquarters, and the coloration was brown, rather than black and white. Hunting drove the quagga to extinction, and the last one died in the Amsterdam Zoo at the end of the 1800s. Museums had preserved skins and mounted specimens, however, so Higuchi and Wilson asked a taxidermist in South Africa to send a mouse-sized clump of quagga skin to Berkeley.

In the lab, Higuchi took a snip of the sample and used what had become a standard DNA extraction protocol. He started with an enzyme called proteinase K, similar to the one used in laundry detergent for removing bloodstains, and another detergent, sodium sulfite, liquefying the quagga skin. He added phenol (carbolic acid is the old name), which removed most materials except the DNA itself.

Genetic samples are sometimes just a few thousand molecules in size; they have to be amplified into a large enough quantity to inspect them. During the early 1980s, the method used to do this was recombinant DNA, which worked by exploiting bacteria. Lab workers inserted genetic fragments into live bacteria, where the DNA replicated on its own, or where it became integrated into the bacteria's chromosome and was copied during reproduction. It worked for the quagga. But Higuchi sequenced only a piece of quagga DNA: the sample was too decayed to do more, and at any rate, with recombinant DNA you didn't know what would be duplicated.

Higuchi's first ancient DNA inquiry, his stunt, fertilized unexpected fields. It created new branches in forensics (old murder cases) and in archaeology (old bones). And it generated big paychecks in entertainment. After the quagga news, novelist Michael Crichton wrote *Jurassic Park,* the big story of dinosaurs cloned from ancient DNA, which Higuchi thinks wasn't so great. "You have to be careful not to overstate what you can do with DNA," he says, "because people are going to view science as an even bigger bogeyman than they do now. It's hard enough to do research because of the Frankenstein factor."

ON THE PHONE, Terry Melton, the hair examiner, had disappointing news. She'd been working on the Aunt Betsy sample, the one belonging to the society writer.

"We tried Aunt Betsy, got absolutely nothing," says Melton. "There's nothing in there. Meaning no DNA. My technician said, 'There's something about those hairs—they just felt hollow.' They were brittle, and they crunched up. Typical of old hair."

Melton sounded frustrated, but accustomed to delivering bad news. She'd given similar reports to police departments.

"We went straight to an ancient DNA approach," Melton says, "looking for one or two small pieces of DNA. In ancient DNA extraction, the idea is to try to recover smaller and smaller pieces of DNA, because it's trending toward breaking up into bits."

Organic materials disintegrate over time, in heat or with moisture. DNA is the same in that the long molecule comes apart, like a rotted rope. For old DNA, labs look for short lengths of the molecule, with fewer base pairs, rather than the big chunks you can get from fresh cheek swabs.

"Our approach with really old samples like yours is to hit it hard immediately, and if you don't get anything, then believe it," says Melton. "Believe that there's nothing there."

TRACE GENETICS, THE PEOPLE steeped in Indian DNA, also called with results. The sample from Isaac Ball had contained no DNA, according to Ripan Malhi, but the other sample, from Isaac's father, had produced a sequence. The mitochondrial DNA in the hair belonging to William Ball was found to be consistent with haplogroup D.

"Haplogroups" and "haplotypes" are like signatures written in the molecule. In mtDNA, some base pairs will differ from one person to the next. A haplo-*type*, a trimming of the phrase "haploid genotype," is the particular set of DNA variations a single individual might possess. A haplo-*group* is more general: a cluster of similar haplotypes, a population set defined by its shared variations. Haplogroup D, the one for William, is one of the population sets on the phylogenetic tree for mitochondrial DNA.

The following fable might illustrate. A family of peasants has a dispute, causing some of them to leave the valley and go over the mountain to live in another valley to the east. Initially, the East Valley branch will carry markers close to those of the West Valley branch; they might share a haplotype. But in time, perhaps 10,000 years, the mutations caused by mistaken copying of DNA will create a split between the two settlements, two haplotypes. To inspect these differences, one can look at the hypervariable regions of mitochondrial DNA, where it is easy to spot tiny alterations.

Haplotype variations are vast and incoherent, so much so that a collaboration of researchers in six countries, the International HapMap Project, has only begun to sort them. Haplogroups are the broader category, variations shared by lots of people. When the accumulation of mutations causes the East Valley and West Valley peasants to diverge at the level of haplotype, they may remain genetically similar enough that they still belong to the same haplogroup, the one that comprises most people in the mountain range. The number of haplogroups is small, fewer than forty, and these are the categories used to map ethnicity.

William Ball's mitochondrial DNA looked consistent with haplogroup D, and haplogroup D, Ripan Malhi says on the phone, is a population signature nearly exclusive to Native Americans.

I MET RIPAN MALHI in Washington, D.C., where he was attending a conference. "Native American individuals," Malhi says, "all belong to one of five lineages, defined by variations in mitochondrial DNA. They're called A, B, C, D, and X. Overall, in the world, there are about thirty-five mitochondrial lineages, or haplogroups. You only find these five in the Americas. They are geographically distributed, so you find haplogroup B high in frequency in the Southwest. Lineage A occurs in places including the subarctic and down the Pacific coastline. And lineage D, which is the one in your hair sample, you find it in the Great Basin, which includes most of Nevada, and you find it also high in frequency in the Southeastern states. It's one of the rarer Native American haplogroups."

Malhi says that his partner, Jason Eshleman, who did the DNA extraction, had taken the age of the material into consideration, "and he became most concerned about contamination on the surface of the hair, so he used a method of ultrasonication to remove it." Although William Ball's hair had produced a sequence, the other sample did not appear to have contained any surviving DNA in it, even though that sample was younger. Malhi says the extraction was repeated to confirm the results, that both procedures ended the same way, "and it wasn't your DNA, either." Labs like Trace Genetics run tests on people who have handled the sample to ensure that the result didn't come from them.

The report said that for William Ball, the relevant variations from the Cambridge Reference Sequence for mtDNA had been at nucleotide positions 16,223 (with a change to base T), 16,325 (C), and 16,362 (C). There was also (at position 5,176) the loss of an *Alu* I site. So-called *Alu* insertions are repetitive sequences about three hundred base pairs long that appear throughout the genome, and the deletion of one of them in the hair sample was characteristic of haplogroup D.

AMERICANUS RUBESCUS, Asiaticus luridus, Afer niger, and *Europaeus albus*: red Americans, yellow Asians, black Africans, and white Europeans. It seems to have been Linnaeus who first characterized the races. Born in Sweden in 1707 as Carl Linné, the son of a Lutheran cleric, and known, other than to Swedes, by his Latinized name, Carolus Linnaeus, he possessed that personality type that thrives on regimentation. Linnaeus studied medicine in the Netherlands before beginning to catalog plants and animals, which would be his life's preoccupation. He created the basis for taxonomy, the scheme of biological classification. His first taxonomy, *Systema Naturae,* came in 1735, and Linnaeus revised and expanded it throughout his life. Bits of his system survive, although not the many names he borrowed from sex, such as his use of terms like *clitoria*, *vulva*, and *fornicata* in the description of plants. Botanists have made an effort to cull these.

As to race, Linnaeus regarded humans as occupying the aforementioned red, yellow, black, and white subspecies.

Because this is the way most people still divide humanity ("Red and yellow, black and white / We are precious in his sight / Jesus loves the little children of the world . . ."), the four branches probably represent the most enduring of Linnaeus's categories. ("Caucasian" was a later term introduced by German naturalist Johann Blumenbach, in the 1790s.)

Native Americans were migrants from Asia. The consensus story, extrapolated from the out-of-Africa model, is that about twenty thousand years ago (the date is in question), groups of people walked into the Americas from East Asia, probably from Mongolia, in southern Siberia, bringing with them the five haplogroups. Geneticists say these travelers crossed Beringia, the land bridge that joined Kamchatka to Alaska during the Ice Age, and they arrived in the New World as small bands of hunter-gatherers. As these bands dispersed into the continent and grew in numbers, they experienced differentiation, genetic drift. From this random sorting, some of the haplogroups rose in frequency, in one region or another, while others fell.

Genetically speaking, there isn't much tribal variation. Navajos do not possess markers that are missing from the DNA of Apaches, in part because people have inhabited North and South America for a comparatively brief time. Sometimes a branch designation allows one to guess tribal affiliation, if a sublineage appeared a few thousand years ago, but the parsing of Indian haplogroups is minimal. About half of the lineages surveyed among Native Americans represent one of the five haplogroups that first came into the hemisphere; the other half represent lineages that developed from mutations after they arrived, broad subsets with names like A2 and D2. The DNA from William's hair, the report said, belonged to a lineage with no postmigration mutations, called basal D.

Ripan Malhi says that haplogroup D also appeared outside the Americas, but that the version shown by the hair could be found only in the Americas and in East Asia, including China and Japan. The possibility of a Chinese or Japanese genetic contribution to an eighteenth-century South Carolina family seemed remote; which left the other explanation, that somewhere there had been a mingling of Native genes. It didn't matter that everyone in the family might be white. All that was required was for one woman, among dozens in the interlocking households of the hair collection, to have come from a tribe. This hypothetical, solitary Indian woman might have lived three to five generations prior to the collectors of the hair. "Or twenty generations," says Malhi.

The way white people might have acquired Native American genes would have been messy. It would have involved circumstances that people name with euphemisms, like concubines, liaisons, and nonconsensual sex. It would have involved power.

If William Ball had carried "Indian" genes, then his mother, source of William's mitochondrial DNA, had given them to him. Eliza Ball had been the woman keen on the aristocracy, on titles, on claiming a coat of arms. Her family, ethnically, had been white; but ancestrally, said the sample, she'd been European and Native American.

5 *Intragression*

ELIZABETH ANNE SCOTT Poyas, "Aunt Betsy," had been a distant cousin, remote enough to strain connection. If I haven't miscounted, our relationship was that of third cousins, four times removed. A faraway relative like this is not so absurd to genetics: one might carry blocks of genes that arrive by a knight's move. I have a copy of a letter that gives an idea of Aunt Betsy's mind. On September 17, 1864, six months before the end of the Civil War, "the Octogenarian Lady" sent twelve pages to William Ball, her grandnephew. Paper had become scarce, due to the blockade of Charleston, so she wrote on scrounged-up stationery from something called the Great Western Insurance Company. White Southerners knew the war was ending, but

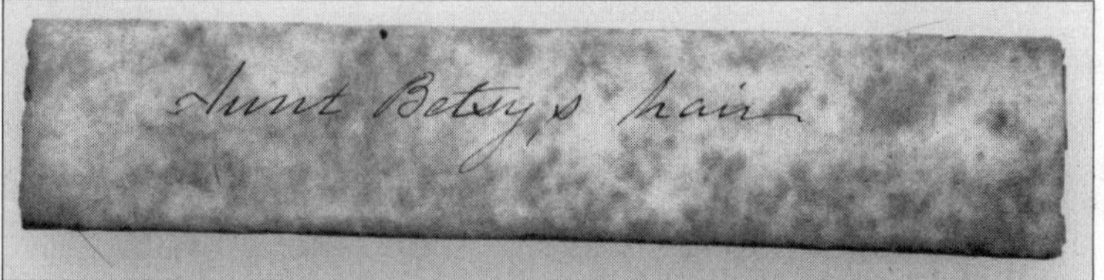

Aunt Betsy wrote letters as though the most important thing was the quaint old days, exemplified in this case by a man she once knew named John Hentie, a land surveyor who used to measure the family property.

> My dear William—And after all I find that you are wishing to know something more of my hero, John Hentie—the freedom-loving, well meaning, but not over-refined friend of many respectable gentlemen and ladies, your own near relations foremost in attentions—whilst he was dividing his favors capriciously from family to family and Parish to Parish, keeping up an interminable warfare at cards, not restraining his fondness for punch and wine. Oh, how many of our high sounding names kept the roadside taverns in those days of his journeying up and down the land as a surveyor, and what a passion he had for fine horses. . . . Permit me then to introduce you to Mr. John Hentie, who was born in 1705, at Rotterdam in Holland, on the 22nd of February. I have traced this man of business through forty-six years of activity and usefulness in the Parishes of St. John, St. Thomas, and St. James Santee, as a merchant, lawyer, and deputy sur-

veyor. He died on the 14th of February 1771, aged 66 years—two days being the extent of his illness.

And so on, for 2,500 words.

In 1812, when she was twenty, Aunt Betsy had married a man named Henry Smith Poyas, a physician as well as her cousin. Both the bride's and groom's families regarded themselves as Huguenots, French people who had emigrated to America. Huguenots were Calvinist believers driven into exile after long persecution in Europe. With hardship and war trailing behind them, Huguenot families felt a survivor's detachment: although Christian and white, they looked on themselves as outsiders. Eliza Ball, like her aunt Betsy, also had the Huguenot story in her past. She'd come from a family named Poyas, the same group as Aunt Betsy's husband, and this fact tied them together.

The Huguenot story was the place where a quantum of Indian blood might be found. The word Huguenot has disputed origins (one comic account claims it was a religious society under the influence of a "Prince Hugh"). Whatever the etymology, these French dissenters had thrived in several pockets within France. They emulated John Calvin, the Swiss Protestant and dogmatist, behavior that made them nonpersons to the Catholic majority, targets for riot and war. Their relative safety ended after 1685, when Louis XIV suspended the Edict of Nantes, which had protected Huguenots from mob violence. Tens of thousands fled to England, and from England they came to America.

In the late 1680s about a hundred families, including some called Poyas, arrived in Charleston, which was then a tiny British outpost intruding on the coastal Indians. English settlers in South Carolina still clung to the port, but the Huguenots, looking for room, moved far from Charleston, sixty miles inland, establishing a village on the Santee River. They were the first Europeans in an area much peopled by Native Americans. Their settlement, Jamestown, didn't grow, and after twenty-five years, the Huguenots acknowledged they'd failed: they moved closer to the main colony and began marrying into English circles. By about 1750, many Huguenot families, like those of Eliza Ball and Aunt Betsy, had merged into Anglican life; but they kept alive their old stories.

Mitochondrial DNA for both Aunt Betsy and Eliza leads back to the Huguenot drama. Aunt Betsy carried mtDNA of her mother, but also that of her mother's mother, going up the mother chain to a woman named Elizabeth Leger, who appears in old genealogies as a French Huguenot immigrant to South Carolina, circa 1685. Eliza Ball, supposed source of the Indian markers, had been born in 1794, and she'd died in 1867. The path of her mitochondrial DNA was this: Eliza's mother had been a woman named Catherine Smith (1768–1836); *her* mother was a woman called Elizabeth Ball (1746–87); *her* mother was named Catherine Gendron (1723–55, another Huguenot); *her* mother was said to have been Elizabeth Mazyck (1698–1785, French Huguenot, and a person who lived an improbable eighty-seven years); and *her* mother was recorded as Marianne Le Serrurier (1675–1732, a Huguenot and a woman thought to have immigrated from France, as a girl, with her parents). According to a 1901 reference, *Family Names of Huguenot Refugees to America*, the name "Gendron" came from La Rochelle, the Protestant city and Atlantic port on the west coast of France; the name "Mazyck" is said to have come from l'Isle de Ré, an island two miles off the coast from La Rochelle; and "Le Serrurier" traces to St. Quentin, on the River Somme, northeast of Paris, in Picardie.

Family trees look tidy, the more so because their purpose is to show respectability. The records of the Huguenots were put down 150 years ago. How much can they be believed?

I would imagine Native Americans and Huguenots, living side by side on the Santee River, shared more than corn and tobacco. "Intragression" is a euphemism in genetics for the blending of populations, what others call interracial mixing. The word appears in stilted sentences, as in, "Caucasian markers intragressed into the East Asian community." But if Indian genes had intragressed into the white population, the event would not have been written down.

MARK SHRIVER, the mind behind DNAPrint, says intragression of all varieties happened in the American past, but family memories were often whitewashed. I visited Shriver at Pennsylvania State University, where he teaches in the Anthropology Department (by chance, in the same town, State College, where hair authority Terry Melton runs her forensics lab, Mitotyping Technologies).

It's Tuesday morning on the big state campus, in a sloped auditorium, a hundred bodies draped on rigid seats for an early class. One student does a crossword, another reads the paper, and a few sleep. In the well, Shriver removes his leather jacket, opens a laptop, and flashes diagrams on the screen. The subject is haplotypes. Shriver projects a map of the world that shows arrows originating in Africa and flowing out around the globe.

"Haplotypes reconstruct the history of populations," he says. "Here are the major migration patterns. We have the origin in Africa one hundred fifty thousand years ago, the spread to different parts of Africa, up into Eurasia, the early move to Australia, into East Asia, and later the move west into Europe. Then, from East Asia over into America, fifteen thousand to thirty-five thousand years ago."

A haplotype, as I mentioned, is a set of DNA variations possessed by an individual. It's a bit like a bar code in that a scan of its features can say much about how an individual fits into ancient human history, or a person's susceptibility to disease. In theory, an individual's haplotype comprises the set of all the single nucleotide polymorphisms that one possesses from each of the two possible alleles (mother's or father's) for a given site on the DNA molecule. In practice, however, genetic variations are inherited in patterns, recognizable blocks of nucleotides that travel together. Testing doesn't let you read the whole genome, only bits of it. But within each block of nucleotides are distinctive alleles that can be read as the signature of one or another haplotype.

The slide dissolves to a diagram that looks like a crowded family tree, with fifty branches tracing back to a single family founder, who, in this case, is a mythic first human population, in central Africa.

"A phylogenetic tree is a common way of analyzing genetic variation," Shriver says, pointing at branches of the chart. "You see that Chinese and Japanese are very close, for all intents forming one population cluster. The branch for African Americans has a feathered structure. And the European Americans—actually, they were first classified as Caucasian, which is a euphemism for white. It's not a good term. It's racialized. It goes back to the way that Johann Blumenbach was thinking about race, or even before him. Although Blumenbach was more advanced than Linnaeus, it brings back the typological thinking about race, with terms like Mongoloid and Negroid. 'Caucasoid' was one of Blumenbach's terms." Shriver steps around the pairing of race and genetics, a combination that anthropology finds difficult to deal with.

"It's rare that you confuse one face with another," he says, "and on the outside, humans do appear to be very different. Despite this, the reality is there is little variation at the genetic level. Just one in a thousand base pairs is different between individuals. The statement that we are ninety-nine point nine percent the same is true."

Someone (Asian) blows a gum bubble up in the seats, and a student (black) randomly aims a camera around the room.

Mark Shriver is the source of population data behind DNAPrint, the testing company that disclosed the percentage of my presumptive Native American genes. His research provides much of the company's revenue, and DNAPrint pays him a royalty from every test it sells.

Shriver's corner of genetics is the blending of populations, or admixture. Away from campus, admixture goes by other names. To journalists, it is "interracial marriage." To white supremacists, it used to be "miscegenation." Geneticists use the neutral term, admixture, a statistical abstraction, not melodrama. Its actors aren't people, but DNA markers.

Admixture, or the mingling of genes, requires genetic dissimilarity, the .1 percent difference. This difference exists because of ancient population movements, as when 40,000 years ago foraging humans in Anatolia split, some migrating into Europe, others to the Indian subcontinent. After separation, the divided populations accumulated harmless mutations, which distinguished them. Following a period of genetic drift, two populations may come together, as when Europeans colonized India in the seventeenth century. Admixture in the children of such reunions makes populations similar again.

Since about 1990, when it became possible to automate DNA analysis, geneticists have cataloged the tiny variations between peoples, nations, and ethnicities. Gradually, gene workers have sorted the world population into the mitochondrial haplogroups, and, beneath them, thousands of haplotypes. Mark Shriver has mined this data and extracted close to 200 of what he calls "ancestry informative markers," sites in the genome that signal where certain genes came from, geographically, and by extension, where someone's predecessors lived. He's published on these markers in journals such as *Genome Research* and the *American Journal of Human Genetics*. Shriver and most geneticists accept that common markers divide people into four general populations: Native Americans, Sub-Saharan Africans, Indo-Europeans, and East Asians. Using Shriver's markers,

DNAPrint tests people for traces of their deep ancestry, and generates reports summarizing the likely ratios of admixture in their DNA. Which is why a fraction of "American Indian" might surface in a white test-taker.

In a boxy 1950s brick building, home to Penn State's Department of Anthropology, Mark Shriver sits at a fluorescent-lit conference table. He is handsome, youthful, dark-haired, and his rectangular eyeglasses are stylish. He has on a navy blue cotton shirt and a necklace made of string and wood. He says he is the son of a scientist and a registered nurse, and that in high school, in southern Louisiana, he knew he'd become a biological scientist of some kind. Shriver graduated in biology from Stony Brook, part of the state university system of New York, on Long Island. He worked for two years in a cancer lab in New York City and got a PhD in genetics from the University of Texas, in Houston. Penn State is his second teaching job.

On the wall behind Shriver hang twenty head shots of past department chairs. The homogenous bunch of men looks like evidence of Caucasian ambitiousness, or maybe preferential success.

Is "race" the outcome of genetic drift, of populations having been separated for tens of thousands of years?

"Race to me is not a biological phenomenon, but a cultural definition," Shriver says. "It's the way we think about ourselves in a sociopolitical context, which is tied up with biology. I've published over fifty papers on human variation, and none of them have used the word 'race.' It's not a scientific concept. Sociologists are more comfortable talking in terms of race, and they can have the word."

The *Oxford English Dictionary* has the word "race" imported from Old French, *rasse*, and perhaps from Italian, *razza*. Before its featured role in human tragedies, the word meant a strain or breed of shared origin, a group of beings (especially cattle) descended from a common ancestor. In taxonomy, the field of category-making, race used to describe a subspecies or variety of a larger group. The 600-year-old word, with its deep roots and bloody associations, is not likely to be expelled from the language. Nevertheless, academics are floating substitute terms, like "population" and "ancestry," which lack the poetic heft of "race." People like Shriver choose these and other words, looking away from the elephant in the room.

Thus far, alternatives to "race" are awkward and wordy. For instance, Shriver's definition of black people living in the United States pirouettes into abstraction. "African Americans are a metapopulation," he says. "They're a conglomerate of lots of real populations and smaller, randomly mating groups." In other words, black Americans, due to centuries of intergroup sex, both voluntary and forced, carry genes from all over the world—West Africa, indigenous America, and Europe.

Scientists may dislike the word "race" (professional journals run editorials that dismiss the term), but the reality is that categories used by geneticists resemble the old racial blocks. When the Ball family collected its hair, in the early 1800s, educated people understood humans to consist of four distinct racial stocks: Indian, Negro, Caucasian, and Mongol.

Genetics has updated this list, but not changed it. The same people who are nervous about "race" apply similar terms to distinguish among populations: Native Americans, Sub-Saharan Africans, Indo-Europeans, and East Asians.

Shriver admits that the population groups fit into the race categories first outlined by Linnaeus, but he says that science also shows these divisions to be fluid, which race theory never does. For example, people with Ashkenazi ancestry often possess markers that suggest Asian or Native American ancestry. In Eastern and southeastern Europe, Shriver says, "you see components of ancestry from Asia, and Native American haplotypes, remembering that such a component could be central Asian." Why would Ashkenazi Jews, or Europeans in, say, Ukraine, possess East Asian markers? One explanation is that Asia, from the Ural Mountains to Beijing, was crossed by ancient trade routes. Ashkenazi Jews who have markers consistent with East Asian DNA might have been linked to the Silk Road trade, which led to mixing between Europeans and eastern Asians. Another reason might be that tens of thousands of years ago, Central Asians drifted in two directions: east toward the Mongolian steppes (and from there to the Americas), and west into Europe. Traces of the root population survive in a few DNA markers.

The science sounds spongy. Except when it doesn't, as in markers associated with malaria. Four DNA variations protect against malaria. (I mentioned one of them earlier, the Duffy-null variation, or DY*0.) The best known of the markers is the sickle-cell mutation of the beta-globin gene, located on chromosome 11. The beta-globin gene codes for a subunit of hemoglobin, which carries oxygen, but the sickle-cell trait, when it's expressed, causes the gene to code for a type of hemoglobin that deforms red blood cells. People with sickle-cell disease have anemia and lots of pain, and about half of them die before age forty.

"The hemoglobin is usually free in the cell, four pieces together floating around," Shriver says. "When you have sickle cell, your hemoglobin gets sticky, and it stretches out the cell into an elongated crescent, like a sickle. If you have one so-called *S* or sickle allele, and one so-called *A* or common allele, in the beta-globin gene, you're protected against malaria. But if your spouse has one *S* and one *A* allele as well, your children can end up with two *S* alleles, and then you have sickle-cell trait. It's an evolutionary trade-off, because the parents are better fit for it, being protected from malaria, and therefore they might have more children." The trade-off being that some of their children will die. The *S* or sickle allele emerged in West Africa four or five different times over the last 50,000 years, Shriver says, with the result that many West Africans carry the mutation. About one in twelve African Americans carries the modified gene.

Shriver has written about the Duffy-null variation, the feature that gives immunity to the *Plasmodium vivax* strain of malaria. Nearly all people in West Africa possess this variation, "and there is no *vivax* malaria there," Shriver says. "It sits on chromosome one, and it's the only perfect ancestry marker we have. Meaning, it's present in ninety-nine percent of Africans, and zero percent of people with no African ancestry. Eighty to ninety percent of African Americans have it, depending on the admixture." Detection of the

Duffy-null mutation, Shriver says, is an unmistakable signal that one has had West African predecessors.

Mark Shriver tells the story that a few years ago, he discovered that he himself carried the Duffy-null mutation. During a study involving thirty blood samples, most of them from students, Shriver noticed that one of the European-American blood donors possessed the Duffy gene. A couple of years passed before he looked at the identification number and saw that it was his own blood sample. By that time, Shriver had taken DNA samples from the rest of his family and had sequenced them all. He found that the Duffy mutation had come from his mother, but that his mother's mother had not carried it. Thus Shriver concluded that his mother's late father must have had DY*0. And, therefore, that he had been a person of African descent.

"Yeah, I believe so," Shriver said. "When you do my analysis it's very consistent with about one great-grandparent with African American ancestry. Which means my mother's family was passing for white for four or five generations, and nobody knew."

Shriver's skin is bright white, and in the Pennsylvania cold, he has rose blossoms on his cheeks. Nevertheless, Shriver says that based on the genetic data, he believes he has "ten or eleven percent" African ancestry. "That's an estimate. It could be half that, or twice that."

America's white population is part African, Shriver says, in that approximately 2 percent of white people, were one to examine their DNA, would be shown, like him, to have some ancestors from sub-Saharan Africa. A bigger proportion of whites, about 30 percent, have less than 90 percent

European ancestry. Such numbers imply that whites aren't as white as they seem, or believe themselves to be. One doesn't hear about this in the discourse on race. It's either unknown, or unacknowledged. In the 2000 census, some 211 million Americans, or about 75 percent, checked the "race" box identifying themselves as "white."

WHY ARE EUROPEANS white, while the rest of the world has colored skin? "The evolutionary explanation combines several things," Shriver says. "Vitamin D is thought to be important. At higher latitudes there is less ultraviolet light, and you need UV to produce vitamin D, so melanin would diminish over time to allow the thinner light to penetrate the skin. Sexual selection is probably another reason. There is more variation in skin color than natural selection can explain alone, and preferences are going to develop about whom to mate with."

Is it possible that those who left Africa to populate the rest of the world were dark-skinned? It's hard to say what the first non-Africans looked like, because skin color has changed tone many times. "The Khoisan people in southern Africa are one of the oldest human populations, genetically, and they have fairly light skin," Shriver says. "However, it does seem that the reason East Asians and Europeans are much lighter than Africans is due to separate events. One of the genes we have that determines skin color has eighty percent frequency in Europeans, and it's not found in East Asians, South Asians, or Native Americans. It's a unique, European skin-lightening allele."

Shriver refers to a pigmentation gene known as SLC24A5. It occurs in many creatures, from humans to inch-long zebrafish. In 2005, the journal *Science* carried an article coauthored by Shriver that described how SLC24A5 codes for melanin production, especially how much melanin goes into skin. The gene allegedly comes in two variants, one common in Africa and Asia, the other widespread in Europe. The versions differ by a single nucleotide, which in turn has an effect on the identity of a single amino acid inserted during protein formation. The European type of SLC24A5 is a mutation of an earlier form, and it contributes to lighter skin by holding back melanin and shrinking the scale of its granules. For all intents, it's a whitening gene.

A SCENARIO FOR my "Indian" genes. A man, a Huguenot settler, lives near the Santee River in the Indian forest, far from Charleston, about 1685. This hypothetical man doesn't have a French wife. He fathers a daughter with an Indian woman. Indian slaves in early South Carolina worked in households more often than they did in fields, and as kitchen workers, they were more likely to be forced into sex with a master. Suppose the hypothetical man then marries one of the French women in the district. Could he and his wife raise his daughter as their own "white" child? The scenario continues. The mixed-race girl grows up and marries into one of the other Huguenot families. None of these events is unlikely, and any of them could have planted "Indian" markers into Eliza Ball's maternal ancestry.

Little of certainty can be said about the women who

came to America a hundred years before Eliza was born. The lives of early American women are twice obscured: once by thin colonial records, and again by being women, who remained legally invisible until they became mothers or their husbands died. No one really knows what women experienced during colonization. Records cite names and dates, but these are questionable, coming as they did from such things as family bibles.

Eliza Ball's mitochondrial DNA would have passed through six women in America. The fifth of the six, Elizabeth Mazyck, stands out. She was said to have been born in 1698 and to have died in 1785, which would have given her a lifespan of almost ninety years, twice the average life expectancy on the frontier, with its untreated disease and epidemic malaria. An implausible luck, such a long life. One way to disguise a family secret—such as a mistress, or an illegitimate daughter—would be to exaggerate the longevity of one person as cover for the taboo of another. Could Elizabeth Mazyck have been two different women, one of whom had intragressed?

Another scenario, this time reversing the sex roles. When they lived in the outland, the Huguenots suffered periodic attacks from Indians. In 1715, a general war between whites and Indians burned through South Carolina, and historical records cite an Indian attack on the French settlements at the Santee River on May 6, 1715, that caused all the whites to flee. If the Indians behaved like soldiers, their raids might have included rape. Could a Huguenot woman have become pregnant from a rape, and, afterward, decided to raise the girl? Twenty years later, this hypothetical daughter would have been marriageable, and with her mother's help, she might have found a way to navigate society. She might have been the strand of Indian DNA smuggled into the white stream.

6 *Kate Fuller*

SOMEWHERE IN A FILE drawer I had a copy of an old photograph, taken about 1890, to judge from the clothes and furniture. It showed a woman in an ankle-length, long-sleeve dress, maybe thirty years old, standing in a photographer's studio against a painted backdrop, the kind meant to suggest a Victorian parlor. She looked at the camera as though it were a reptile. Until the DNA test with Native American results, I'd forgotten about the picture, and it may have been an unconscious suppression, because the photograph appeared to be another clue to the family's ambiguous racial identity.

The woman's name was Kate Fuller, and she was my father's maternal grandmother. She'd lived in Charleston with her husband, a man named Theodore Porter, in the late 1800s, and she'd died at age thirty-six, leaving behind five children, including my father's mother. A cousin had given me the picture. "The family of Kate Fuller were from Edisto Island," the cousin had said, "and before that, it was rumored they were from Barbados. I think she looks like a mulatta."

The faintly obscene word, *mulatta*, meaning a woman with one black and one white parent, became common during the Colonial period, when whites and people of color made children in large numbers. As vocabulary, *mulatta* brings to mind an older America and its race scale, when blood quantum had legal status, and "one-quarter Negro" was a term used by the federal government. The noun *mulatto/mulatta* comes from Spanish and translates as "mule." No one uses it anymore.

The woman in the picture was my great-grandmother. Had she been mixed-race? Comparing her picture to photos of her husband and other family members, Kate Fuller seemed to have had sepia-toned skin; her lips look thicker than "white" lips, and she has a flattened nose. Her hair, pulled back, looks wavy, maybe kinky. Then, too, when you look for these things, your eyes exaggerate them, or invent.

Everyone has sixteen great-grandparents, and all of mine were dead by the time I was born. There was no one around to ask (assuming anybody would have given a straight answer), "Was she colored?" One-sixteenth of an individual's genetic composition equals about 6.25 percent. If Kate Fuller had had a white father and a black mother, and if her mother had been nearly "pure" African, then, in theory, her great-grandchildren would be one thirty-second (3.125 percent) "Negro."

Sources said that the Fuller family to which Kate belonged had lived, during the eighteenth century, in the town of Beaufort, South Carolina. The Fuller home still stands; it's known as Tabby Manse, an unusual house with walls made of oyster shells, lime, and sand. One of the progeny, Richard Fuller, had become a Baptist preacher, converting from Episcopalianism during the revival that swept the country in the 1830s. After that, a branch of the family had moved to nearby Edisto Island. Edisto was one of the sea islands and about 90 percent black until the 1950s. Kate Fuller had come from the Edisto Island branch. I could find nothing more on Kate, no record of her childhood, only her tombstone at Magnolia Cemetery in Charleston, where she lay buried next to her husband, Theodore Porter.

Kate Fuller and Theodore Porter had been my father's maternal grandparents, but I don't recall him ever speaking of them. He talked a lot about Theodore Porter's father, Anthony Toomer Porter, a man who had founded churches and schools, a man prominent in the way people would like dead relatives to have been. My father might have had three reasons that he didn't talk about his mother's parents. First, and most likely, they'd both died by the time he was five. Second (also likely), one of them had been mentally ill (my father's grandfather, Theodore, whose story I'll get to). A third reason he didn't mention them might have been that my father's grandmother, Kate Fuller, wasn't entirely white. Then, as now, the standard in force was that one drop of black blood meant you were African American.

Kate Fuller's hair didn't appear in the collection from the old desk. Despite this, was there a way to examine her DNA, a way to look for African markers that might have been "forgotten"?

In 2000, the U.S. Census Bureau started to count people who checked more than one race box on the population form, but at the same time, the agency declined to create a new category of ethnicity. (The word proposed, but tabled, was "multiracial.") The data, at any rate, were chalked up. That year, 6,826,228 people, or 2.4 percent of the population, chose to associate themselves with two or more races. Of these, 1,082,683 people, amounting to 0.4 percent of Americans, called themselves white and American Indian. A smaller group, 784,764, or 0.3 percent of the nation, said they were white and African American.

It was unlikely Kate Fuller had been mixed-race. She'd lived in the South after Reconstruction, when whites took segregation seriously and when interracial marriage was banned. Interracial sex took place—it happened all the time, mainly between white men and black women—but a taboo remained against interracial marriage. No white family would knowingly have allowed a son to marry a woman of color. Which means that the alleged mulatta Kate Fuller couldn't have just appeared in white circles, ready for courtship, without someone talking about her parents.

No, Kate Fuller couldn't have been mixed, furthermore, because a DNA test had uncovered my supposed Indianness, but it had shown no genetic markers from West Africa. Wouldn't her African-ness have left some trace in me, one of her third-generation offspring?

It might, and it might not. Genetic markers travel in bundles, and gene transmission is like gambling. Because of recombination, the shuffling of genes when egg and sperm join, unless both parents possess the same markers, you might receive one set of variations, and a cousin gets another. Which meant it was theoretically possible for one person to possess West African markers, while a close relative does not. Also, ancestry tests include an error margin of about 3 percent. Small percentages of admixture can be overlooked.

Tests from other family members help to clarify, so I got in touch with a cousin, Catherine Tupper. Catherine had grown up in a town near Charleston called Summerville, where her father had run a gas station, and we'd known each other since childhood. Catherine's mother and my father had been siblings, and when we visited South Carolina, our family stayed with Catherine's in their big wooden house on five acres. Both Catherine and I were great-grandchildren of Kate Fuller. On the phone, I described the hypothesis, and the science. Catherine wasn't surprised; she'd been the person who'd given me the photo of Kate in the first place, saying "She looks like a mulatta." Catherine wanted to find out more, and she agreed to DNA tests. The outcome might settle whether we were white, or "white and some other race."

THE SMOKY MOUNTAINS rise in western North Carolina, where white fog spills down lumping hills, and the loudest noise comes from preachers shouting in their pulpits. The mountains are summer refuge for people from the Carolinas, so it wasn't surprising when Catherine Tupper moved up from Charleston.

Catherine was one of the cousins I'd looked up to when I was growing up. She was older and knew things like how to saddle a horse, and her brothers knew where to swim versus where to fish in the creeks. At fifty-five, Catherine remained 110 pounds, stood about five-five, and spoke with a rubbery Carolina accent, one-syl-la-ble-at-a-time. She made the dialect her own with an idiosyncrasy, which was to stress the final word in each sentence. "If I have Indian genes, nothing would please me *MORE*," she said on the phone. She lived in the gentler Appalachians, east of Asheville, where you can drive through two or three pocket valleys in ten minutes. Her rented brick ranch sat in a dip across from an abandoned farmhouse and a dairy farm, a few miles from the tourist stop called Bat Cave ("the largest granite fissure cave in North America").

Bob Faires, Catherine's not-the-first husband, had grown up in the same town and gone to the same schools, although the two didn't notice each other until middle age. Each had children from previous marriages, a circumstance that provided sidecars to their relationship. Bob was a former State Police officer and after that a carpenter who could frame a house and build cabinets while watching the news. The couple had replaced their children with a cat and six dogs—three Boykin spaniels, a golden retriever, a terrier, a bulldog—all rescued from impoundment, overweight, and deranged with energy.

Catherine wore a lavender-and-black turtleneck sweater,

black pants, and gold hoop earrings; the eyeglasses on her face were round and the diameter of oranges. Her short brown hair, full lips, and unwavering eyes reminded me of her mother, as did her temperament, reserved until something broke the mood, at which she yielded to a flood of laughter. Her husband, Bob, was stocky and shaven bald, with a dark mustache that wrote a thick line across his face. He spoke more slowly than Catherine, who herself meandered, so that together they clocked about sixty words a minute.

Catherine brought out her original of the photograph of Kate Fuller, and the hundred-year-old print looked new.

"The dress was maroon color," Catherine says. "My mother had it, and she also had the earrings she's wearing in the picture. Mother gave the dress away and sold the earrings, when she sold a lot of things to send my brother to school. I suppose you could have checked the earrings for DNA."

Bob says, "I'm convinced if you go back far enough, everybody came from the same two cells, originally."

"Kate Fuller's mother had lived at a plantation on Edisto Island, which burned," Catherine says. "And by the way, I was named after Kate. She was my mother's grandmother, but the spelling was different. It was Katherine, with a K."

Catherine mentions another picture of Kate, "in which she looks one hundred percent Caucasian." She produced it, a close-up portrait.

"A hundred percent?" Bob says, shaking his head. "Does not look that way to me. Not at all. Look at the texture of the hair." Catherine laughs, discharging the nervousness.

"And now they go in and get these injections to make their lips bigger," said Bob, "but in this picture, her lower lip is fairly heavy. And look at her nose. But it doesn't make any difference."

Catherine's house was a hybrid, the modern plainness given texture with old pictures and old furniture: an Empire chest, a china cabinet with convex doors, daguerreotypes of family members, a photograph of Catherine's mother wearing a mantua.

"We have a secret drawer in one of those pieces of furniture," she says. "Also, my mother had a collection of hair, but she'd discarded it. The hair had come down through the Ball family, and it was wrapped in what looked like rice paper. One of the locks was reddish in color." She was describing another group of hair mementos, a doppelgänger to my own.

Midday dinner interrupted—shrimp salad, red rice, baked ham, squash casserole, asparagus, beets, pecan pie, and ice cream—during which the six dogs, each in turn, tried to jump over the gate that kept them in the kitchen.

Catherine had agreed to have her DNA analyzed, and she said she was surprised when members of her family had complained. At first she'd thought they'd spoken up because tests might reveal a disease propensity that could, if disclosed, sabotage health insurance. But disease linkages don't surface with ancestry tests. She thought there was another reason. "Only the Balls think they're pure Caucasian," she says, and laughs.

I'd arranged for DNAPrint to send Catherine a cheek swab kit. Results had come back, and I handed her the ancestry data. The report contained a summary of her DNA's "ancestral proportions," and this sentence: "Test results suggest that your ancestry is predominantly European in origin with significant East Asian/Native American and Sub-Saharan African ancestry in your genome." A table gave numbers. "European—85% ancestry . . . East Asian/Native American—11% ancestry . . . Sub-Saharan African—4% ancestry."

The test on Catherine's cheek swab said she possessed "white" genetic markers, "Indian" variations (the third test in the family to do so), and a small black African genetic contribution. The results were consistent with an incident of "race mixing" five generations ago.

That there might have been a Native American in the family tree looked increasingly possible. And the great-grandmother Catherine and I shared, Kate Fuller, the presumptive mulatta—the source of the sub-Saharan 4 percent? If Kate Fuller had been "one-quarter black," in the jargon, then three generations later, her progeny could be 4 percent black, give or take a point.

Catherine looked at the page. "Four percent black, and eleven percent Native American," she says. "Oh boy, I wish my father were alive."

"Who says two hundred or three hundred years ago someone didn't marry out of the fold?" Bob says.

"Someone evidently did," Catherine answers. "Mother said that her grandmother, whom she called Munnoo, insisted that they leave the plantation and move into Charleston. That would have been about 1890. The reason Munnoo gave was, she said, 'I don't want my children to marry Indians and darkies.' To even suggest it, coming from her, this could have happened. She must have heard of it, somewhere."

"Families remember what they want to remember," Bob says.

"Another thing my mother always pointed out was that I had the derriere of a black child," says Catherine.

"Like an apple butt," says Bob.

"That's crass. She always said I had a derriere like Brenda Branton's, but I wasn't allowed to play with Brenda in Summerville. Because Brenda's family was mulatto."

It couldn't have been easy for a person with Native American or African ancestry to marry into the family. At that time, 150 years ago, the racial system was set to maximum sensitivity, and people knew more about the families they married into.

Bob was less skeptical. "Go way back," he says. "There were probably gold diggers back then, too. And several generations later, instead of 1710, maybe in 1810, the features may be more acceptable."

Bob, the former highway patrolman, his perfect mustache combed downward, mentions his own family. "My grandfather was a full-blooded Indian," he says. Catherine turns. "Yes, Bob. Sometimes I look at you and think you look like Genghis Khan."

This was a genetics joke. Bob's shaved head made him macho, and he and Catherine knew that "Native Americans" had migrated from Mongolia across the Bering land bridge. "Half Mescalero Apache and half Hopi," Bob says.

"From New Mexico. His name was W. R. Faires. He ran away when his mother died, and his father had already died. Eventually my grandfather wound up in California, where he became a rancher and a builder, and a licensed architect. Built schools and highways for the state of California. And he married a woman named Elsie Garner, who was the sister of the vice president of the United States—Roosevelt's first vice president, John Garner. My grandfather died in 1963, and he had all his property sold, and he left everything to different Indian reservations."

The story of Bob's grandparents, a Native American marrying the daughter of the vice president, sounded like marrying up, in genetic terms, streaming genes from one class pool to another. In two pictures, Bob's grandfather indeed appeared to have been two men, a worker on horseback in chaps, or a squire, an urbane figure in white suits.

I mentioned that Trace Genetics, the California lab, had extracted DNA from one of the hair samples and had assigned the sequence to haplogroup D, a Native American set. There'd been several tests with overlapping results.

Catherine thought the tests had revealed something hidden. "I wonder who these women were in these family trees, where they had no last names," she says. "Were they Native Americans? These young Englishmen who came alone to the New World, we just think that they came with these lovely English brides, but you just know they must have married into the indigenous population. If you just didn't talk about it, the next generation didn't learn about it, and the information was lost."

Bob says, "I've read history where it was almost a chic thing to do to marry what was thought of as an Indian princess."

"You know those young men on the frontier didn't live celibate lives," says Catherine.

But there was something uncertain. The equations behind the test put the admixture numbers into a likelihood interval, to use the mathematics term. The report said it was "ninety percent likely the number was correct" and "two times less likely" the number was wrong, that Catherine's sequence contained nothing from West Africa. In other words, there was a high likelihood it was true, and a middling one that it wasn't true.

Bob turned to Catherine. "Look here." He pushed his finger on her nose to make it flat, then laughed. "Apple butt."

THE TESTS RELATED to Kate Fuller had been of Catherine's and my nuclear DNA. An additional screen, of mitochondrial DNA, might settle the business of black admixture.

Kate Fuller had been Catherine's mother's mother's mother. Since mitochondrial DNA passes down from mother to daughter unchanged, Kate had conveyed her mitochondrial sequence to Catherine. To test Catherine's mtDNA would be the same as testing Kate Fuller: the result wouldn't be diluted by recombination.

I brought out a buccal swab kit. Catherine removed the stick from the sterile paper and scrubbed it on her inside cheek.

"I'll never be able to go home to South Carolina," she says. "I'll have to stay up here in the mountains."

We walked out into her backyard, with a view of the rolling hills.

"DNA is pretty accurate stuff," Catherine says. "Otherwise they would never put anybody in jail with DNA evidence. And they wouldn't exonerate people who were sitting on death row, if they weren't pretty sure of the science."

7 *The Color of Home*

When I was a child, I had freckles on my cheeks and down my arms, and I didn't like them, especially after kids started calling me Spot. My mother had freckles, my brother and father didn't: they stood on one side of the family, physically, my mother and I on the other. They were thinner and squarer, whereas we had bigger noses and were flabbier. I didn't like my wavy hair, which was also my mother's, dark curls hard to get through with a comb. My brother's hair was straight, and Dad's hair had been straight before he went bald. Mornings before school, to master the curls, I put on Brylcreem, a head lacquer that immobilized frizz.

On my palms is the blotchiness of my mother's skin, and

on my hands, her freckles. A crook in my middle finger was my father's. These are templates taken from my parents, maintained by a million nucleotides, traits replenished uncountable times by new cells, replicas, as the old ones die. The body is the twin of consciousness, its existential home, but the thought of occupying a continuous replica of one's self gives it nauseating strangeness.

When I was the boy called Spot, we lived on a chip of land next to Charleston called Sullivan's Island, where I bicycled to school every morning. In a few blocks, there came a beat-up wooden house, home to a skinny blond kid named Randy. He was mean, as was his dog, an obnoxious, underfed thing whose name I've forgotten. As I came along, Randy, in his door, would say, "Sic 'em!" and the mutt would run for my bike. Randy would later appear on the playground at school, smiling.

Our school stood next to the sand dunes, and on windy days you could hear the crash of the surf from the other side, the Atlantic Ocean churning. The wind came over the dunes to blow up girls' dresses and to tangle my hair, creating an Afro. An Afro was not a desirable thing in an all-white primary school in the South, especially at a time when black people were wearing big hair.

Our science teacher was Mrs. Charles, who was black. As the only Negro on staff, with the exception of the janitor, Mrs. Charles was on hand to demonstrate that integration was proceeding with due speed, even though it had been about twenty years since the desegregation order had come out of the Supreme Court of Chief Justice Earl Warren.

Mrs. Charles was more formal than any white teacher. She dressed in heels and stockings, compared with the naked knees and flats of the white women. She owned five or six suits, and I would mentally check them off, guessing which she'd wear next morning. Mrs. Charles's hair was conked and frozen in a bob, she smiled about once a week, and she used precise, exaggerated diction, hitting all the syllables ("Ev-er-y at-ti-tude mat-ters"). Her skin was very dark, her temperament like a high-tension cable. She gave the impression that something bad had always just happened to her, and that she might snap before the last bell.

Something else set Mrs. Charles apart. She'd arranged her classroom on a diagonal, a disorienting floor plan that might have liberated the space were it not a strenuous expression of Mrs. Charles's difference. Students faced a corner, not the blackboard, and you had to turn your head to the right to watch the teacher.

Mrs. Charles was the person fate had arranged to give our class of twenty-five white ten-year-olds a first lesson in genetics. It's surprising that any knowledge of DNA had trickled down to a primary school in South Carolina, a state in which some voters regarded evolution to be a dimension of Communist propaganda. But there it was—"*Ev-o-lu-tion,*" as Mrs. Charles said in her verbal italics, writing it all the way out.

"Break it down into syl-la-bles," Mrs. Charles said.

"D-N-A," I said. Too many syllables in the real word.

"No," said Mrs. Charles. "The en-tire word."

A few kids muttered, "Dee . . . oxy . . . new . . ."

"*De-ox-y-ri-bo-nu-cle-ic* acid," said Mrs. Charles. "D-N-A."

The boy with the obnoxious dog said, "No way! The first part is, like, *duh. Duh*-oxy!" Another kid laughed, then someone else said, "The *Y* is long, like ox-*eye*!"

The genetics lesson spiraled off and got louder. The class talked all at once about whether the *E's* were "ee's," and whether *nucleic* should be pronounced "new-clee-ic." Mrs. Charles slapped a ruler.

"Children!"

She closed her eyes and kept them shut. Maybe it was the strangeness of it. Of all the voices on behalf of science, she'd been chosen to tell these noisy little white children about their genes.

FOR SOME YEARS while I was growing up, our family lived in south Florida, enough time that sliding glass doors glide back and forth in dreams. Our backyard stood about equidistant from the Everglades, to the west, and Cuba, to the south. One fall, in the public school I attended, a teacher organized a class trip, and perhaps because the Marxist state was off-limits, we went to Everglades National Park. The purpose of the trip, said the teacher, was to see the "real Indians" who lived in the park.

The Everglades were wetlands that used to run 300 miles from the middle of Florida to its southern tip, but they'd been bulldozed into orange groves and subdivisions, leaving a rump and retreating marsh. The remnant was beautiful, a lake to the horizon with three-foot waves of grass, alligators thrashing, and solid clumps of island covered in mangroves. Sportsmen crisscrossed the shallow idyll in fan-powered airboats as loud as jets.

The Seminole Indians had been native to Florida, with a population of 100,000 or more until the invasions of Spain and England, in whose civilizing embrace they met the usual fate of subjugation and mass death, concluding in a holding pattern of alcoholism. When Florida became U.S. territory in 1821, Southern farmers pushed down from Georgia, and deportation ensued, with quisling Seminole chiefs moving their people to Indian Territory, later known as Oklahoma. Thousands resisted, and American soldiers descended to extract the holdouts in the Seminole War of 1835–42. A few hundred Seminoles escaped, left behind in hideouts in the Everglades. In late-twentieth-century Florida, their descendants numbered about two thousand.

When our class visited, the Indians were shaking out a living from tourist points in the Everglades called Seminole Villages. No one actually lived in these places: each comprised a few grass huts, to which Seminoles arrived in battered cars to spend the day behaving "like Indians." When the school bus pulled up at our chosen Seminole Village, a few dark-skinned people with long hair got out of folding chairs to occupy the huts. We entered one to find that it was a trinket stand. I remember talking to an indifferent man who smoked and parried questions behind his card table, from which he sold key chains made from swamp cypress and necklaces that dangled rubber alligators. The man's face was dark, his hair stiff and long; his moccasins looked new and had perhaps come from Taiwan.

The teacher called us to the dusty square between the huts, and five Indians rose with much avoidance to perform a dance, loping around in a circle to bells and drums. I remember that one Indian woman, overweight and inappropriately dressed—her suede jacket and turquoise bracelets were the costume of the Southwest—cut into the scene's grimness with her laughter. She talked a stream, made fun of the dancers, and neglected her table of doodads. Her black hair shined, and the arrival of another school bus didn't break her monologue, which she punctuated with sips from a bottle. For a fee, our class could have stayed to watch the afternoon show, which was to be a man wrestling an alligator in a pit. We wanted to wait, but the teacher disapproved.

Aside from being someplace to distract public school students (we were mostly white, a few Cuban), the value of the Seminole Villages seems to have been to demonstrate the proper attitude that we future citizens were to assume toward the state's natives. I remember the inflections of the grown-ups, which signaled the correct and contradictory emotions. Seminoles were thought to be many things: pitiful, interesting, to be avoided, dirty, artful, in touch with the marsh, and, somehow sadly, no-longer-what-they-used-to-be. I remember the teacher's lament that, instead of digging out tree trunks, the Indians bought metal canoes. She had little to say about how they'd gotten to the rubber alligator stage.

It was my first encounter with Native Americans, and it chiseled a perspective. For many years, the Seminoles, in my mind, were the model for all Indians: they were different from us, with benighted lives best seen from a bus window.

My mother's family had come from New Orleans, and in their history I know something about two family names, Rowley and Lecorgne, one of them English, the other French. Neither group would wish to be found carrying the Duffy-null marker, the DNA variation that signifies you have African ancestry. The degree to which this would be unwelcome might be seen in the behavior of my mother's great-grandfather, a man who possessed the melodic, baroque name of Polycarp Constant Lecorgne.

Of his extraordinary name, I know that Constant and Lecorgne were surnames imported from France. Polycarp had been the name of a Christian martyr in Smyrna during the second century. Polycarp Constant Lecorgne had been my mother's mother's father's father. He was said to have been a second lieutenant in the Civil War, a flag-bearer who served a few months in Virginia before returning home. Later, according to lore, he and a friend walked up the Mississippi River levee to Jackson, Louisiana, where the two enlisted in the so-called Thirteenth Trans-Mississippi Regiment, an outfit that Polycarp seems to have preferred to the one in Virginia, since he didn't desert it, and he served till the end of fighting.

After the war, Polycarp kept up the rebellion. Reconstruction included the occupation of Louisiana by a victorious army, which left many whites with a contempt for northerners and did little to dissolve the old dislike for black people. In New Orleans, whites hated Union occupation, more so after a black governor took office. Some whites tried to do something about the infamy of "Negro rule," and one of them was Polycarp.

In his middle years (by which time he and his wife, Gabrielle Duchemin, had had nine children), Polycarp joined a militia known as the White League. Formed during the 1870s, the White League succeeded an earlier insurgent movement, the Knights of the White Camelia; both mobilized old Confederates to engage in subterfuge and violence. The White League targeted black people in authority, as well as liberal whites, and it differed from the Ku Klux Klan in that it wasn't a secret organization. In Louisiana, the League became the main supremacist front and drew more militants than the Klan, leading an uprising against Northern occupation and engaging in battles with Louisiana's state militia, which was mostly black. At night, members of the League would ride their horses through black villages, shooting in the air, sending the message that white rule would be restored, and it would be sharp.

White League vigilantes stalked and killed black leaders, and its mobs killed several black state legislators. Among their white victims was a politician named Marshall Harvey Twitchell, a former Union captain from Vermont who ran a branch of the Reconstruction agency, the Freedmen's Bureau, in Bienville Parish, in northwest Louisiana. Twitchell had married the daughter of a local planter, but this didn't alter his status as a carpetbagger from the North who helped black people. In 1874, while Twitchell was in New Orleans, White League militiamen killed his brother, two brothers-in-law, and three other white Republicans. Two years later, the League came back to kill Twitchell, who survived, but lost both arms in the attack.

My mother's family lore reports that our good predecessor Polycarp Lecorgne was a soldier in the White League. It is remembered that he took part in the decisive confrontation, the Battle of Liberty Place, in New Orleans, on September 14, 1874, when the New Orleans Metropolitan Police, an integrated militia of 600, backed up by 3,000 black state militia, faced White League units numbering several thousand. Eleven police died, with sixty wounded; sixteen White Leaguers were killed, and forty-five wounded, including Polycarp, who "had his head split open," according to the family story. After the battle, which took place in the center of New Orleans, the Union occupiers of Louisiana decided to give up and leave. Reconstruction ended, and white rule returned.

Polycarp lived another decade. He died in 1886, apparently after drinking contaminated water on a hunting trip.

I never heard directly about Polycarp's private war, either from my mother or from anyone else in her family. But my mother had had an aunt, an unmarried schoolteacher named Maude Lecorgne, who, after retirement, wrote down some family history that she'd absorbed. It was in Aunt Maude's genealogical notes that I first encountered the supremacist legacy of Polycarp.

GENEALOGY, A SEARCH for family history, is practiced by millions of middle-aged and middle-class Americans, for whom it has traditionally been a way to snatch a bit of glory or a helping of fantasy from the past. It is, after all, the little activities, visiting libraries and surfing Web sites, that allow anyone to acquire "good genes." Most people who do family research are white, and most of them look for ancestors with the goal to unearth the whitest, most moneyed forebears they can. That is one definition of good genes.

White people are said to be unaware that they are white, unable to see their whiteness as an ethnicity, but I don't believe it, because as a child, I knew we were white and pure. It was like a good smell. My parents knew their kids were growing up in white enclaves, a normal and desirable thing. A few times my father countered our isolation by taking us to black churches to worship with "them," but in fact we watched how "they" did it. In the South's smaller places, before about 1965, there was no embarrassment in talking about "the white race." Words like "Aryan" and "Caucasian" have since become taboo, perverse jokes, but I remember adults using the words without choking.

Aryans (Sanskrit, "of noble birth") were the mythic former inhabitants of northwest India, who by legend moved west and became founders of Europe. (The racial legend has an odd parallel to the story of migration in the out-of-Africa model.) German naturalist Johann Blumenbach coined the word *Caucasian* in connection with the Aryan story of origins. It referred to the myth that Aryans were supposed to have arrived in Europe via the Caucasus Mountains, northeast of Turkey. The Caucasian subplot detached white Europeans from their Asian roots (what white person wanted to be from India?), and it added moral baggage to the birth of whiteness: it was said the Caucasians survived their journey across harsh terrain in a mountainous and cold, remote place, bringing vigor and enterprise to the quest of founding Europe and the white race.

The same Johann Blumenbach used comparisons of skull shape and size to show supposed Caucasian uniqueness, inventing craniology, an early racial science. Craniology gave way, in the nineteenth century, to anthropometry, an early tool of forensics that cataloged such things as finger length and foot size, correlating them with class and color. A version of racial measuring has surfaced again in biometrics, the basis of a security industry that reads people with scanners.

My parents, aunts, and uncles didn't talk about Caucasians and Aryans, but the words were around. All the newspapers, the school forms to be filled out, all the television reporters used "Caucasian" as adjective and noun. White supremacists used "Aryan" in the flaky pamphlets they left at bus stops, fliers dotted with spelling errors. Most whites ignored the supremacists, who were ranters and people who'd quit ninth grade, but their ideas didn't seem alien. Our race had a heroic past, flickering dimly, casting a long shadow.

Once, when I was about eight years old, my parents went on a bank errand and took me along. They were visibly nervous, because the errand was to break my father's paycheck; this was something they never did, but of late they'd had medical bills. The teller counted out $500, my father's monthly salary. My mother, who had worked as a bookkeeper, counted the money again, with reverence, and folded the bills into her wallet. From these few minutes, I took a permanent impression about money, the substance that could make one's parents, godlike adults, grip the armrests of a chair in anxiety.

My father, an Episcopal priest, brought home an unexorbitant income, which paid for one car, the one in which we took our vacations because airfare was too high. Our housing was on loan, the property of the church. One summer, as a gift to the collection plate, a member of my father's congregation, who owned an appliance store, outfitted our house with the bewildering luxury of central air-conditioning. My mother clipped coupons and carried a bundle of them on trips to the grocery. My parents had no inherited money, and they owned no stock.

But the intangibles. Proximity to the church gave us social value, and the game of family background meant a lot. It was a marker of some kind that both my parents possessed old family stories; that their people had ended up in the same cemeteries for centuries. As a child, I knew that our origins could be traced to northern Europe, and that the adjective "northern" conveyed an extra measure of status. The ability to locate one's predecessors in England or France was regarded as virtuous, because northern Europe was regarded as an almost utopian place.

My father had come from a string of Protestants, and while some of my mother's family had French names, and were Catholic, my mother's branch was not. Then, as now, blond hair was a marker of goodness and desirability, and we were one down on that chart, because no one was blond. But there were a lot of tall people, and some had "Nordic" features: chins, cheekbones, high foreheads. The term was obsolete but still somewhat in play, and it didn't sound strange to hear adults speak of "their Nordic line."

No money, but cultural capital. Sometimes, through the cloud of our meager circumstances, I couldn't see it, but in time the outline of our good fortune was plain.

THE PICTURE SHARPENED in the years we lived in Florida. We moved there when my father was assigned a church in Miami. Our house, the rectory, was a flat-topped, 1960s three-bedroom with sliding glass doors and a big lawn. The setting must have alienated my parents, who hailed from unmodern New Orleans and Charleston, but they gamely mowed the lawn and made Jell-O. Some Saturdays, my parents would take my brother and me out to sample the Florida culture. Usually we'd go to the beach, but sometimes we'd go to a new section of town, Little Havana.

It was 1965. Five years previous, the Cuban Revolution had pushed out the dictatorship of Fulgencio Batista, and Miami had been filling with exiles. They arrived on weekly "Freedom Flights" and moved into Little Havana. The exiles were often middle-class, people with clean fingernails, but to people like us, they were exotic.

On a sunny afternoon, Dad would ease the Chevy Impala (white, with a red vinyl interior) into a parking spot about a block from the main street in Little Havana. The four of us would disembark and begin a walk up the sidewalk. We'd move slowly, listening to Spanish (talk was loud here), studying the clothes (billowing shirts, primary colors). We'd eye the espresso stands, the stores selling statues of saints, the lunch places where they squashed cheese sandwiches in the window. We huddled together, a school of fish led by my father, negotiating the reef of wedding shops, Santería stores, little groceries. Eventually we'd stop to buy something small, a snow cone. This, too, was alien, because the man scraped the ice off a huge block on a cart and poured sticky syrup from a dirty bottle. My mother would take my hand if we encountered something inexplicable, such as men playing dominoes on the sidewalk. In the reflective glass of the storefronts, we could see ourselves edging past, and we saw what we weren't, as well as what we were.

8 *Cousin Marriage*

THE SPINDLIEST ASSORTMENT of hairs, fifty or sixty half-inch strands, carried the most laconic label—"John Ball." I knew who he was from the handwriting, which I'd seen on at least a hundred letters, most of them about money. John Ball was the manager in the group. He'd been drafted into the role after his father died, in 1817, and then his brother, Isaac, in 1825, the deaths making John the guardian of no fewer than seventeen half-sisters, half-brothers, nieces, and nephews, in addition to his own children. For a decade, John spent a couple of days a week answering demands for money, trying to see to it that all the fatherless family had something. He disliked it, but he'd been a dutiful follower and the responsible one all his

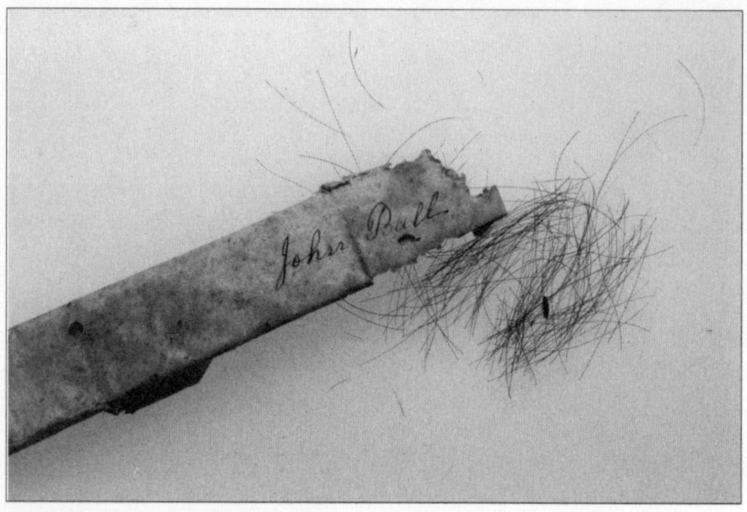

life. I recognized the handwriting, but I also knew that John had been nearly bald. Thus, the spindliest hair.

John Ball was oval-faced, with eyes closely set and an expression of mild but continual fear. In his portraits, his lips look pursed, as though from a lemon. He was the older brother of Isaac Ball, who'd started the hair collection and who had probably asked for a lock during one of his brother's frequent visits (the two lived a few blocks from each other). John was the more introspective and smarter sibling. When he was eleven, he was described by an uncle as a boy "with a very meek disposition." As an adolescent, the timid son signaled to his parents that he might become a minister. Disappointed, but disguising it, John's parents packed him off for a trip to England, where they hoped he would outgrow his piousness during walks on the Strand.

Returning to America, John took schooling from an

English tutor named Benjamin Slade, whom his parents had paid to follow their son home from London. John's brother, Isaac, was Slade's other, decidedly more casual student, but confident where John was shy. John listened to Slade, Isaac didn't. Isaac never attended college; at age sixteen John enrolled at Harvard.

When he arrived in Massachusetts to start school, in fall 1798, John still hadn't surrendered the idea of the clergy. One of his teachers, noting his studiousness, told John that since he might one day be a bishop, he might as well learn Hebrew. John wrote home to his father that he was thinking of Hebrew, an idea that struck his father as daft. "Yes I am glad you have an oppty to learn Hebrew," John's father wrote back, "yet I would have you try to pronounce & speak French well, because it will be more useful to you in your travels." The son had poor social skills ("your diffidence," his father called it), and Hebrew would not open doors in places like French Louisiana, and Paris.

John's uncle, Elias Ball III, the man who'd commissioned the secretary, possessed a certain influence over him and offered an enticement to pry the boy away from the church. Come home and get a wife, the uncle told his nephew, and I'll give you a reward. The advice came in a letter John's uncle sent to him: "Marry your cousin Betsy Bryan and I will settle you at Comingtee"—Comingtee being one of the family plantations with a high income.

Finishing at Harvard in 1802, John returned to Charleston and did what he was told; he married his cousin, Elizabeth Bryan, daughter of his father's sister. It may have helped that she was quiet, like her husband. The couple moved to the plantation promised to them. Five years passed before John's uncle gave them title.

As was custom, John and Betsy lived between their plantation, a day's trip from Charleston and amid hundreds of enslaved workers, and a house in the city, where they mixed with whites. John's town house was modest compared with his brother Isaac's. The more gregarious and showy Isaac had built a big mansion; two of its parlors could swallow John's house entire.

John's wife Betsy died young, in 1812, at twenty-eight, probably of malaria. Eighteen months later, John remarried, to a woman named Ann Simons, the daughter of a family from which other relatives had already extracted spouses. During his middle years, John looked after his brood of dependents, but by the 1830s, the tribe was mostly grown. He had more time, and the freedom led him to make a bad choice: he decided to enter politics. John had never shaken his social awkwardness, and he likely was a fumbling speaker. It came as no surprise to those who knew him that he lost his first campaign, to join the state legislature. Aiming lower, in 1832 John got himself elected to the Charleston City Council. Perhaps if he'd lived, John would have claimed a bigger role than the one that resulted. When he become a politician, the fight over states' rights had just begun. John attended the political conventions where the subject was being argued, and he began to position himself for a place in the coming storm. The states' rights movement in South Carolina would one day launch the Civil War.

But, like so many before him, John contracted malaria. He died in June 1834 at his plantation, Comingtee, at age fifty-one.

JOHN BALL'S MARRIAGE to his cousin, Betsy Bryan, brings to mind the old habit of Southerners to mate with their own. Within minutes of first meeting a northerner, a person from the South of a certain mentality, fond of cliché, is more likely than not to make the observation that, "We're all related down here." Nervous laughter may accompany this remark. The same individual, alone with his own regional kind, might refine his truism into a joke about its real subject, which is incest. He might add, "We're all related, because we all have one leg shorter than the other."

It's true that families in the South once practice inbreeding. The memory of this fact gives rise to neurosis south of Virginia, nasty gossip elsewhere. Cousin marriage became taboo in the early 1900s, but it was common until that time, when something happened to dampen the enthusiasm for it. Within the families that collected the hair, I counted twelve cousin marriages between the years 1750 and 1900. Eight of them took place between first cousins, four between second. (First cousins married the child of their uncle or aunt; second cousins had grandparents who'd been siblings.) Two cases stand out. During the 1860s, three sisters (last name, Poyas) married their three cousins, named Ball. In these marriages, two of the three grooms were brothers, and the third was a son of one of those brothers from a prior marriage (which had also been to a cousin). The triple-cousin assemblage appeared in the family of William Ball, whose hair was the first of the samples.

The second case shows how cousin marriage made people lackadaisical about finding a mate, an assignment most approach with interest. In the late 1850s, John Alwyn Ball, a three-year-old boy in a family close to the brothers, John and Isaac, lost his father to illness. The three-year-old's mother, a woman named Caroline Rutledge Ball, recovered by marrying a man named Frederick Fraser, a widower with two children, including a daughter named Emily. The families merged, and Emily and John, the stepsiblings, grew up together in the same house in rooms situated across the hall from each other. When John turned twenty-one, in 1876, he and his stepsister Emily decided to marry. Their parents did not object, and the marriage took place. In their search for a spouse, the couple had not left their own second-floor hallway.

Anthropologists call marriage inside the tribe or clan endogamy. Southerners did not regard endogamy as a repellent practice, but one that made financial and social sense. According to those who practiced it, including several within the hair collection, the custom of marrying inside the fold derived from sexual scarcity, a shortage of suitable mates. But this was a tautology: the alleged scarcity derived from a cramped understanding of suitability. A suitable mate had to escape many exclusions. One could not marry people who worked with their hands; or shopkeepers; Jews, Catholics, immigrants, or blacks. The small pool of eligibles that remained was further winnowed by class and geography. A suitable partner had to come from a family that owned a plantation, as well as lived within a day's travel, so that cousins could go home to visit. For people in the hair collection, the criteria cut the list to about twenty households within twenty miles.

Endogamy must have saved time and trouble, because partners didn't have to master the politics of their mate's family (since it was also their own). This aspect of coupling can take years, and it can go badly.

Scarcity might have been the advertised motive, but the true incentive for cousins to marry was to protect the money. Until William Ball's generation, the family had wealth and didn't want to lose it. Setting up with a cousin meant conserving the inheritance. It isn't coincidence that inmarriage stopped when the money was gone.

IN THE LATE 1800s, Francis Galton, a British author and a cousin of Charles Darwin, brought to life his most famous creation. He proposed a social movement called "eugenics," a word he'd coined meaning "well-born." Galton regarded himself as a reformer who merely wanted healthy people to have more children. Eugenics failed in Britain, but succeeded in America, where it was reborn as a negative cause, a drive to discourage "unsuitable" people from proliferating.

Elites in Northern states led the eugenics movement, many of them working from a compound on the Long Island Sound at Cold Spring Harbor, fifty miles east of New York City. This fishing cove became home to the Eugenics Record Office, founded in 1910 and run by a biologist and crusader for "race betterment" named Charles Davenport. At the head of a cadre of anti-immigration reformers, Davenport mobilized a politics of race superiority, putting out publicity and pushing legislation that targeted "shiftless" and "feeble-minded" people for harassment and possible sterilization. Cold Spring Harbor operated as a racist hub. Staff members compiled population data on subjects like "Jews and nervousness," "race crossing," "race and hair," "cousin marriage," "Caucasian Mountain Whites," and "family idiocy." The aim was to stratify and catalog, with the goal of sifting out undesirables. Within twenty years, eugenicists had convinced millions that heredity caused most social problems, from alcoholism, to "pauperism," mental illness, "imbecilism," and criminal behavior; and that managing the flow of genes should be a government priority.

Eugenics was the other thing that changed the attitude of Southerners toward marrying their cousins. Beginning about World War I, propagandists from the Eugenics Record Office and similar groups traveled to Southern states to admonish people that they'd been doing something wrong with their genes. Lecturers visited health departments, legislatures, and prison bureaucrats, sweeping from Louisiana to North Carolina, making the case for controlled mating. Cousin marriage came in for special disdain. Many Southern politicians embraced the new portrait of heredity and race and pledged allegiance to the cause. Thirty states passed eugenic sterilization laws that compelled "imbecile" and other menacing women to undergo tubal ligation. More than 65,000 sterilizations were achieved before World War II, until Nazism shamed doctors who chose to engage in court-ordered tube-tying.

The war silenced the eugenics movement. Afterward, the institute at Cold Spring Harbor shed its association with sterilization and compulsory warehousing of "defectives." The Eugenics Record Office disappeared, seamlessly replaced on the same grounds by a center for DNA science. Cold Spring Harbor Laboratory, rededicated to molecular biology, has scant memory of its eugenic past. At any rate, geneticists insist the story is irrelevant to what they do.

EVERY FAMILY HAS a genetic identity, made up of a unique toss of genes. Usually, people refresh their DNA by throwing it in with the different genes of partners. But when a family marries itself, the mixing slows, and there are fewer genes to toss.

A well-known cautionary tale about inmarriage involves Queen Victoria, who carried a gene associated with hemophilia. In 1840, the young queen married one of her first cousins, Francis Charles Augustus Albert Emmanuel of Saxe-Coburg-Gotha, Duke of Saxony, the future Prince Albert. Hemophilia is linked to a recessive gene, which steps aside for the other parent's dominant (healthy) gene, until by chance it encounters another recessive hemophilia gene carried by a fertile partner. When that happens, the two recessive genes make an expressed trait, which is hemophilia.

Albert and Victoria had two daughters who carried the hemophilia gene, and one son with the disease. These children married their cousins, and *their* children married *their* cousins, until Victoria's demure, recessive gene had been fortified, multiplied, and recombined, allowing the disease to flourish, so that within two generations, the queen's descendants included six hemophiliac men.

One of Victoria's granddaughters, Alix Victoria, a hemophilia carrier, married the last tsar, Nicholas II Romanov, and that couple had a son, Alexis, affected by hemophilia. It was said that Rasputin, the Siberian mystic, gained access to the Romanov court because he seemed to be able to offset the boy's bouts of bruising and bleeding.

The family of Charles Darwin also observed a vigorous schedule of cousin marriage. In 1838, Darwin married his first cousin, Emma Wedgwood. The groom's father, Robert Darwin, had married into the same family, to one Susannah Wedgwood. Further, Susannah Wedgwood (Charles Darwin's mother) had been the daughter of a cousin marriage between her parents, Josiah and Sarah Wedgwood.

Josiah Wedgwood, Charles Darwin's wife's grandfather, was the originator of Wedgwood pottery. The Wedgwood firm made plates and tableware for the rich, a consequence of which was that the Wedgwood women came to their Darwin husbands with large resources. Charles Darwin did not have to work: he lived in a spacious house near London (not grand, a farmhouse on a village main street, but nevertheless with servants and acreage), had money for a family of ten children, and wrote and traveled. The fruit of cousin marriage.

Three thousand years ago, the author or authors who wrote the book of Leviticus put down a taboo against endogamy, which has run through Jewish and Christian life. In Leviticus, chapter 18, the prohibition states, "None of you shall approach to any that is near of kin to him, to uncover their nakedness . . ." The text bans intercourse with one's mother, father, uncle, aunt, and a numerous list of other relatives.

The proportion of cousin marriages in the Ball family was less than half, but over time, children married repeatedly into the same seven or eight families, which had a multiplying effect. The whole group stayed within a radius of ten miles, and they went back to the same chromosomal well for partners (a few surnames repeat in the marriage records, like a metronome), creating conditions like those of an isolated, island population.

Did cousin marriage have genetic consequences, as the eugenics movement warned that it would? Were there repeating DNA mutations sustained by endogamy? Circumstantial evidence says there were. Hereditary blindness caused by glaucoma zigzags down the family tree. My father had glaucoma, and during his twenties, the disease blinded him in the left eye. A great-uncle of his had it, as did his grandfather, who went completely blind late in life. In genetic terms, my father and his grandfather had two conditions: adult-onset glaucoma and early-onset open-angle glaucoma. In 2000, a lab at the University of Iowa College of Medicine made the case that adult-onset glaucoma associates with a mutation in a gene called GLC1A, on chromosome 1; whereas the early-onset form, according to a different study, in 2004, links to markers on chromosomes 9 and 20.

There have been other family ailments, including depression. I agree that posthumous diagnosis makes questionable medicine, but one can detect depression in remembered behavior and in the letters that people leave behind. A more conspicuous story, though, involves a history of mental illness that ran for generations, when over several decades in the early 1900s, my father's family developed a reputation for "madness."

It started with my father's maternal grandfather, a man named Theodore Atkinson Porter. The stories about Theodore Porter are thin, because his derangement continued to cause shame in the family long after he died. Born in Charleston in 1885, Porter followed the path taken by his father, an Episcopal priest, and he was ordained in the ministry about 1880. Later, he took the job of rector at a church his father had built in Charleston, called Holy Communion. But in the 1890s, Theodore Porter's wife, Kate Fuller, suddenly died, at age thirty-six, leaving him several young children. A year or two later, gossip traveled that Reverend Porter was becoming detached from reality. (One wonders about the sermons.) He was forced to resign, an event described in church records as "the rector's illness." Reverend Porter's dementia grew until other family members chose a typical solution for the time, which was to remove him from society. Such was the euphemism for the kidnapping of loved ones deemed unable to manage. Bundled away, Theodore Porter, clergyman, father of young children, was confined to an attic.

This part, the true gothic detail, bears repeating: Reverend Porter was locked in an attic for many years. The attic was situated in the rafters of a building on the campus of Porter Military Academy, a boy's high school founded by

Theodore Porter's father. Here, during his forties, Reverend Porter, the crazy man under the eaves, paced the floor and stared out of the window. I should point out that in Charleston, before air-conditioning, an attic was like a furnace.

I had a cousin who remembered, from her childhood, the demented man who sat in his upper-story window, looking down to the street. The madman in the attic couldn't come down, because at street level were the boys of Porter Military, who taunted him until he would be forced to run back to the stairs.

Theodore Porter's siblings eventually moved him to the state-run lunatic asylum, a quasi-medieval institution a hundred miles from Charleston in the capital city of Columbia. At the time, the mental hospital employed minimal treatment, probably consisting of physical restraint, plus food. After about ten years, Reverend Porter died in confinement, alone and neglected.

Theodore Porter had a daughter, Theodora, known as Tido, whom he loved. She was a girl of about ten when her father began to lose his mind. Tido apparently inherited her father's genetic predisposition to mental illness. Tido also went mad, and she was also put away in the same lunatic asylum where her father had spent his last years. She passed decades in the institution, and Tido also died incarcerated, like her father had before her.

Tido Porter's derangement occurred in the 1940s, by which time medicine possessed a diagnosis. She was labeled "schizophrenic." According to the fourth edition of the *Diagnostic and Statistical Manual of Mental Disorders*

(*DSM*), the playbook of professional psychiatry, schizophrenia can have various subtypes and phases; but diagnostic criteria for the central disorder include two or more of these symptoms: delusions, hallucinations, disorganized speech (frequent derailment of thought, incoherence), grossly disorganized or catatonic behavior, and so-called negative symptoms, such as flattening of affect. The *DSM* claims that first-degree relatives of schizophrenics have ten times the risk of the disorder than the general population. It does not name the genes that might be relevant, which haven't been convincingly isolated.

It is impossible to say what had been wrong with Reverend Porter, Tido's father; but his condition may have been related to hers. Had the mental health profession existed in the 1890s, Reverend Porter might also have been diagnosed with schizophrenia.

Tido had a sister, Susan Magdalene Porter, who was my grandmother. I remember Granny as a woman with an elliptical face and plump lips, a gray-white bun of long hair, and a preternaturally quiet disposition. Granny's clothing style was premodern (dress to mid-calf, floral patterns, stockings). Children remember the odor of adults, and to me Granny smelled like a tree, musty, mossy, and moist.

Granny was old when I was a child, and I remember her as a withdrawn, minimally expressive woman. When she laughed, it was usually a polite laugh, and extremely brief. Granny sat for hours on the sofa, laconic, watching her grandchildren, reading and rereading the paper. She seemed to want all drama to take place far away from her, without her having to be involved. She was weak and used a cane.

Maybe she was tired, or maybe it was depression. Circumstances had been cruel to her.

Granny's behavior is no longer mysterious, as it was to me then. Her mother, Kate Fuller, had died when she was seven. Her father had gone mad a few years after that and remained locked in a stifling attic while she was growing up. When she was in her thirties, her sister had developed schizophrenia. Eventually, both her father and sister were sent away to die in the same warehouse of the insane.

It may be relevant that Granny's family, the Porters, practiced endogamy, though perhaps not as assiduously as William Ball and his group, who married one another a dozen times.

THE GENETICS OF mental illness are not well described. Genetics puts much emphasis on the adaptive nature of mutations: if a mutation gives rise to a trait that spreads, then it is likely that the new gene has some adaptive value. But what is the adaptive use of dementia, or of depression? Hallucinations would seem to lack adaptive value.

Still, a calculus of sorts can be made about the risks of cousin marriage. First-cousin couples (who share one set of grandparents) possess one-eighth of all their genes in common. If these married cousins carry a (detrimental) recessive gene, then the likelihood of a harmful gene pairing in a child amounts to one in sixteen, a risk far greater than that for children of unrelated parents.

Cousin marriage is nearly gone from Europe and America, partly because of the legacy of eugenics, but the desire to find a partner in one's own family and perpetuate the clan remains common around the world. According to the World Health Organization (WHO), in the eastern Mediterranean (Turkey, Egypt, Lebanon, parts of Greece), between 20 and 50 percent of marriages take place between blood relatives. In Europe and North America, the number is fewer than one in a hundred. Health agencies refer to it as "consanguineous marriage" (meaning, "of common blood"). The WHO has concluded that first-cousin marriage doubles the total frequency of congenital and genetic disorders, and that more than one generation of endogamy multiplies the risk of recessively inherited disorders fifteen to thirty times.

According to the Centers for Disease Control, seven regions for possible "schizophrenia genes" have been identified. (Their approximate whereabouts, as expressed in cytogenetic location notes, are 5q11–q13, 11q14–21, 6p24–p22, 22q11–q13, 6q13–q26, 8p21, and 13q32.) But there is no genetic test for schizophrenia, because no one has demonstrated that such genes exist. The most that can be expected in the medium term is further groping by clinicians. A 2004 study of bipolar disorder among Ashkenazi Jews provides a typical instance of psychiatric genetics, the field where the schizophrenia issue now resides. The study looked at forty-one families with bipolar disorder and decided that most patients had a high incidence of variation on chromosome 18. An interesting finding, but not conclusive.

Mental illness, for me, remained a hidden family story. Probably there were madness genes rattling at the bottom of the family tin, but the instruments didn't reach deep enough to find them.

9 *Poisoned Children*

LYDIA BALL BRYAN must have looked pretty good in her eighties. Her contribution—"Aunt Cingie's hair age 82"—was silky and auburn-colored and came tied in a string. Dyed and packaged: one assumes Lydia used henna and whatever else to keep the years off.

She was a great-aunt of William Ball and had watched him grow up from a four-year-old who'd inherited Limerick plantation to a new father, in 1842. Lydia apparently visited William and his wife, Julia, when they were first-time parents and had resumed the hair collecting left off by William's father.

The nickname Aunt Cingie might have been a child's attempt that stuck (Lydia = Cingie?). She hadn't had time

for her own childhood, at any rate. She'd been born Lydia Ball, on a plantation called Kensington, in the late 1750s. Her parents parceled her out. In 1771, when she was fourteen years old, she was married to a man named Edward Simons, twenty-nine. A stepsister of Lydia's had married Edward's older brother, and the parents decided to make it a symmetrical foursome: two brothers, two sisters. If Edward Simons was a groom with some property, he was none too rich, being one of thirteen children in line for his parents' money. Edward and Lydia, the child bride, moved to Charleston, where Lydia gave birth to their son, Edward, when she was fifteen.

The boy died an infant, and, two years after that, Lydia's husband also died, leaving her alone. Events turned colder still when Lydia discovered the contents of her husband's will, drafted just before he died. It ordered that all the couple's belongings be sold, save a few of Lydia's personal things, which he specified: "the Gold watch, equipages and appurtenances which she has in use." With no place to live, at age eighteen, she went back to her parents, traumatized.

Eight years later, Lydia married again, at age twenty-six, to a widower named John Bryan. His deceased wife happened to have been the sister of Lydia's dead husband, a maudlin connection, but one that reveals again the tight circle of potential mates. (At least they could talk about their former partners.) Lydia's new husband was an immigrant from England who'd been in America five years. He'd acquired a plantation, called Camp Vere, and a workforce consisting of about fifty slaves. Lydia and John moved to Camp Vere, situated across the river from Lydia's birthplace, and Lydia had two children. One of them, Elizabeth Bryan, would eventually marry back into the Ball family. (She was Betsy Bryan, wife of the meek John Ball, the woman in the admonition, "Marry your cousin Betsy . . .")

In 1803, Lydia's husband John Bryan died, at age fifty-one. This time, instead of a gold watch, Aunt Cingie kept her house in Charleston, where she lived for a widowhood that lasted another forty years. In the 1840s, she came to the living room of William Ball, her grand-nephew, to deposit a lock of hair. She was in her eighties, had outlived most of her generation, and she was still paying social calls.

IT'S A SURPRISE, in a way, that Aunt Cingie had survived at all, since the collectors of the hair had to endure a good deal of awful medical care. These were the years of bleeding and of mercury cures, both of which lowered already scant life expectancy. Other dubious treatments included opium, administered for a variety of ailments.

Aunt Cingie and the rest used medicines that would later become subject to felonious possession. Account books in the family contain pharmacists' charges for quantities of laudanum. One of the earliest manufactured drugs, laudanum consisted of a bottle of alcohol suffused with opium. Letters from family members show that they took laudanum for intestinal pain and fever, and they gave it to their children to make them sleep. (They didn't give it to their slaves, perhaps because it was expensive.)

Their opium use fit the prevailing taste. Until the early 1800s, prosperous whites consumed raw opium, a nasty brownish paste, as a remedy for pain, diarrhea, and fever. The drug relieved symptoms, but it also altered the mind, imparting well-being, calm, and mild hallucinations. As a solution, easy to spoon, laudanum offered an improvement on raw opium. To make it, a pharmacist took the raw material, the Asian poppy, cut a wound in it to bleed out the sap, boiled that, skimmed off the solids, and reduced the fluid to a paste. The paste was melted in alcohol to make the tincture. Throughout the nineteenth century, the family consumed steady quantities.

It occurred to me that Aunt Cingie, an old woman, perhaps a person in need of pain relief, might have used the drug. The thought grew when I came across an article in the *Journal of Forensic Sciences,* in which an examiner named William Baumgartner claimed to have found opiates in hairs from the head of John Keats ("five hairs, 7.6 cm in length"). Tests apparently showed the poet had used laudanum as he was dying, in 1821, of tuberculosis.

In the case of Aunt Cingie, my curiosity would be disappointed. I first contacted a criminal forensics laboratory, the Institute for Legal Medicine, in Münster, Germany. This was the crime lab used by the German national police in drug cases. The lab director was an affable, thirtyish man—blond, towering, gentle—named Carsten Hohoff. He agreed to examine Aunt Cingie's hair. Two months and several reports later, Dr. Hohoff sent results showing no trace of opiates. Perhaps it had been wishful thinking, or maybe the drug had broken down during 100 years in the desk. Or maybe Aunt Cingie, of teenage motherhood and hennaed hair, was a woman who had taken life stoically.

"Isaac Ball, aged 4 yrs" was not the vain Isaac Ball who'd preened around the city in his phaeton. He was, however, that man's namesake, and his grandson. Born in 1844, this younger Isaac was the second child of William and Julia Ball, occupants of Limerick plantation, which they'd inherited from William's father, the first Isaac Ball. At age four, little Isaac surrendered a long blond lock to his parents, the only blond hair in the group, so pale as to look Nordic.

When Isaac was a boy, his life alternated between strict lessons and easy adventure. At age nine, he went off to New York City with an uncle—they took a steamboat up the Atlantic coast—just for the boy's pleasure. Writing home to his mother, Isaac talked of the music and theater he'd seen, and he was excited enough to leave all punctuation out of his letters. Back in South Carolina, Isaac returned to the grip of his private tutor, a twentysomething graduate named Matthew Davis. The tutor reinstated Isaac's punctuation and also taught him classics and mathematics, subjects imparted to sons, though not to daughters. Isaac's full childhood thinned, however, when he reached his teens, and his mother, who'd been ill for years, died at age thirty-five. Isaac and his three brothers were thrown into the considerable ranks of single-parent children.

It may have been connected to his mother's death that at this point, Isaac took up music. He studied the violin. His father had played guitar in his youth, and his aunt Jane played a majestic-looking harp, if not beautifully, then without embarrassment. Isaac's brother Willie took up piano; and a cousin, Aunt Jane's son John Shoolbred, played cello. In a couple of years, Isaac was leading all of them in chamber music soirées after family dinners.

At seventeen, Isaac enrolled in South Carolina College, the same school his father had attended, a day's rail trip from home. His life plan also resembled his father's: a few years at school, and back to the plantation business. But the Civil War broke out when Isaac was a freshman. Young men felt they had to prove themselves, which meant the week he turned eighteen, in 1862, Isaac quit school and enlisted in a Confederate unit, joining his brother Willie, the pianist, who was already in uniform.

The city of Charleston had come under siege, and the teenagers (Willie was nineteen) were posted to an island fort at the mouth of the harbor, with Union troops camped a mile away. Isaac, an artilleryman, lobbed missiles that kept the invaders away from Charleston. When the city finally fell, in February 1865, he marched with his unit as far as North Carolina, fighting in the last skirmishes of the rebels. In a wartime notebook, Isaac described the surrender as tersely as possible: "27th [April]—Guns turned over to the Quartermaster in Greensboro."

At age twenty-one, a war veteran, his future as a plantation squire trimmed by the defeat of the South and the emancipation of his family's slaves, Isaac returned home, where evidence suggests he fell into a depression. His aunt Jane wrote a friend, "I don't know yet what Isaac will get at, I hope he will find occupation and not wear out his life." Isaac went back to school to finish his interrupted education. Three years later he was done, the question of income unanswered. He had three brothers also at home, and his father was selling off the land.

A future came in the form of a wife. In 1869, Isaac married Mary Louisa Moultrie, heiress to a rice plantation called the Bluff. Isaac moved to the 1,200-acre tract to live with Mary Louisa and her mother. He'd become something like his father after all, operating the Bluff with black sharecroppers, dividing the annual rice harvest with the workers, rather than taking it all, which was the old system.

In 1880—Isaac was thirty-six, his wife thirty-three—there were six children, aged one to ten. According to census records, there was also a large domestic staff ("nine servants, 3 of them under age 10"). Mary Louisa ultimately had twelve children at the Bluff, one of whom was my grandfather, Nathaniel Ball. The family stayed on the land until 1892, a bad year for the rice crop, after which they moved to Charleston and found a house to rent.

During his middle years, Isaac Ball was a rice planter, church vestryman, father of a multitude, joke-teller, violin-player, and sometime poet. His personality seems to have had two sides. He was a commanding storyteller, with a gift for character and love for plots that ended in reversal. (His ironic narrative style can be seen in a book, *A Day on Cooper River,* spun largely from the wool of his stories.) He was also damaged by the war, with a shock of loss that never faded. Though he'd survived three years in uniform without physical injury, Isaac had been so marked that, fifty years after the fighting, he was writing sad little poems about the Confederate cause.

Unlike his stories, which entertained, Isaac's poetry might be described as an artifact. None of it was published; it survives in notebooks, most of it sentimental war verse, his personal medicine. One poem, "Of the Old Guns," says, in part:

While we did this port defend
Stern Fate decreed a bitter end.
O'erwhelmed by hordes on many a field
Our thinned gray lines at last did yield.
Our human masters may forgive
But in their hearts fond memories live.
They love to fight their battles o'er
And talk of scenes and days of yore. . . .
Yes, in a righteous fight they gave
Their lives for land they tried to save.

Isaac outlived his wife, Mary Louisa, by seven years. In his last decade, he went blind from glaucoma. He died in 1933, at age eighty-eight.

ISAAC BALL'S HAIR was one of the locks that contained no DNA. I'd sent it to Trace Genetics, the company that had found "Indian" markers in William Ball's sample, but no genetic material in that of Isaac, his son. The blond locks were plentiful, however, so I decided to subject them to other forensic tests.

Forensic toxicology, historians of crime say, began with a test on human remains performed in 1836. James Marsh, a chemist working at the Royal Arsenal in Woolwich, on the Thames River downstream from London, devised a way to detect arsenic in soft tissue. Arsenic had become a murder weapon, and the military chemist was interested in the use of the poison.

Invisible and discreet, poisoning had long success as an elite crime, a killing method preferred by the rich to the knifings and shootings of the volatile poor. Until the 1900s, any customer at a chemist could buy hemlock, belladonna, or mercury salts: professional poisoners earned a good living in secret, even as their tools were sold in open air. So obvious was the trade, however, that arsenic trioxide (which James Marsh would find in his flesh samples) acquired the name "inheritance powder," because its application was known to speed the transfer of wealth between generations.

An investigator in Germany first thought to look for traces of poison in hair. The case unfolded in Frankfurt in

1858, when a chemist found arsenic in the hair of a body exhumed after eleven years. The result seems to have cheered the police, because hair analysis for toxins remains a protocol in some labs.

As far as I knew, the likelihood of an arsenic murder in the family was small. Common sense also said that Isaac, a four-year-old, was not likely to have suffered toxic exposure. Those who collected hair samples lived on fresh-water farms in the country, supposedly clean places. The South stayed with farming, pristine and healthy, as the Industrial Revolution overtook the North, yellowing the rivers with effluents and contaminating the cities. For these reasons, a toxicological exam of Isaac's hair would certainly turn up nothing.

Commercial laboratories offered toxicity analysis, and eight or ten labs examined hair alone. I sent strands of Isaac's hair to one in Texas called Trace Elements.

There are four elements whose presence in the environment one might worry about: arsenic, lead, mercury, and strontium. (Better-schooled people worry about more.) Ingested in tiny amounts, all cause health problems, from neurological decay to cancer. Heavy metals and other elements find their way into hair in a mechanical way. Lead travels in the blood, and traces of it stay behind in the hair root. The bits get trapped in keratin, the protein that makes up the hair shaft, and remain there during growth. In this way hair becomes a chronicle of what a person has ingested, an inch of hair recording about a month of body chemistry.

Most chemists lack a fistful of curls belonging to long-dead relatives and the curiosity such a thing provokes. But in 1989, the journal *Biological Trace Element Research* reported an attempt to measure average element levels in hair. The study, by the Centers for Disease Control (CDC), the government arm that quantifies illness, took hairs from 271 American adults, aged twenty to seventy-three, ran them through analysis, and came up with figures. A microgram (µg) is one-millionth (0.000001) of a gram. It's the unit used in many public health warnings, as in, "The minimum risk level for intake of polychlorinated biphenyls, PCBs, is 0.03 µg/kg/day." The mean quantities of the four dangerous metals present in hair, measured in micrograms per gram of prepared solution, were said to be 1.1 µg arsenic, 2.12 µg lead, 3.55 µg mercury, and 3.4 µg strontium.

Trace Elements (different from Trace Genetics, the DNA lab) said that it used atomic emission spectrometry (AES), a process that measures the presence of metals in minute concentrations. In AES, the sample (hair, but it could be anything) is placed in solution and heated to high temperature, 8,000 Kelvins (14,000 degrees Fahrenheit). At this heat, the solvent evaporates, and the temperature is raised again until the solid material turns to ash, vapor, and finally into atoms. When the energy source is cut, these atomic bits decay to status quo. While cooling, they emit light, and this is when traces of elements show themselves. All the elements present in the sample will emit light at the same time, but each element sends out a different spectrum. The presence of an element like arsenic or lead is signaled by the appearance of its signature wavelength. A wavelength detector reads the light and records its wavelength, while a different device senses the intensity of the emission and determines the quantity of metal present.

The report on four-year-old Isaac's hair contained a surprise. It suggested that the boy had been subjected to huge toxic doses.

According to the CDC reference values, the mean presence in hair of methylmercury, the form of mercury retained by tissue, is 3.55 µg. Isaac had 11.6 µg, or 3.27 times the norm. Things were worse with arsenic. The mean for arsenic was 1.1 µg for people not environmentally exposed to it. Isaac Ball's hair showed 5.12 µg, or 4.65 times that amount. The highest numbers came in lead. Isaac's level measured 917 µg, or 433 times the mean. The toxicity report came with a graph that mapped the results from the hair against the company's own references, which differed slightly from those of the CDC. In mercury, arsenic, and lead, Isaac's concentrations were so high that the values were off the chart.

One of the four toxic elements, strontium, showed an acceptable range (2.2 µg in Isaac's hair, against a mean of 3.4 µg for late-twentieth-century samples). Strontium-90 is the radioactive isotope of that element, the risky kind. As the result of nuclear accidents and bomb tests, small amounts have spread everywhere. (The isotope has a half-life of twenty-nine years.) It made sense that hair from a century before Hiroshima would not be heavy with strontium.

Of the other three toxins, the ones with unchartable numbers, arsenic is a carcinogen that encourages skin, lung, and liver cancer, and prolonged ingestion can cause anemia, confusion, and convulsions. Mercury accumulation in tissue debilitates the nervous system, and it's been linked to tremors, memory loss, and ataxia (poor muscle control).

And one characteristic of lead poisoning is stippling, round, dark-blue granules in the red blood cells.

I DID NOT EXPECT toxic-dump levels of pollution in my collection of remains, and so, to widen the sample, I turned to the sample for "John Ball b1825 d1852."

This John Ball was not the dutiful businessman who'd taken on guardianship of seventeen children. In fact, he'd been one of those seventeen, an infant at the death of his father, Isaac Ball. When his hair was collected, John Ball was a twenty-six-year-old landlord. I sent the sample for toxicological assessment to a company in Chicago called Doctor's Data.

John Ball had been the last child of Isaac and Eliza Ball, the parents who'd originated the hair collection. I mentioned earlier the painted miniature that shows his handsome, dark, sculptural face. Although plenty of records illuminate the lives of John's brother, William, all I could find about John's childhood were a few facts about his property, and notes about a trip abroad.

When he was not yet one year old, John inherited a plantation, Hyde Park, plus another tract near the Limerick family house. These things were to be managed by accountants until the boy reached twenty-one. John remained close to his mother throughout his life, and their trip to England together in 1845 sealed their bond. This was the trip in which they saw bathing cars attached to horses, which pulled swimmers into the water; the trip that took Eliza to the College of Arms on a vain search for a family title.

John's is the only hair that appears twice in the collection, and this, too, involved his mother. When he was a boy of five, in 1831, Eliza had cut off a lock. Perhaps he was sick, and Eliza thought he was headed for the grave, like her first two children. The second time Eliza cut his hair, in July 1852, John may indeed have been deceased, stretched out in bed. He'd died of fever, malaria, leaving a wife and two children. I imagine John's mother cut the second lock from her son's head to add it to the first, two mementos from the boy she'd loved, the son who'd followed her around in her widowhood.

WHEN JOHN BALL DIED, according to the new toxicity results, his body was full of poisons, even more so than his nephew, four-year-old Isaac. Lead seemed to be the main contaminant. John's hair contained about 1,400 µg, or 700 times the reference values for lead set by the Centers for Disease Control. (A note from the lab technician read, "Insufficient sample to recheck results," which meant that the tech couldn't believe the readings.)

The CDC, a branch of the Department of Health and Human Services, had published an advisory on lead exposure. It stated that a blood test that showed 10 micrograms of lead per deciliter (dL) was judged to be worth medical or legal investigation. John Ball's 1,400 µg was equivalent to 56 µg per dL, or nearly six times the threshold of alarm.

According to the Environmental Protection Agency, a blood lead level between 10 and 30 µg/dL in children can affect hearing and growth. At blood levels between 40 and

70 µg/dL, anemia occurs. Reports of neurological symptoms and impaired nerve conduction have been seen in people with levels of 40 to 60 µg/dL; and at 80 µg/dL, the kidneys and brain are irreversibly damaged.

The two poisonous strands of hair—John's and Isaac's—had come from the same household. John Ball had grown up during the 1820s and '30s in the Limerick plantation house, and in the family house in Charleston. Isaac had grown up during the 1840s and '50s in the same two houses. Lead in drinking water has been attributed to lead pipes, solder, and fixtures, and it may have been that the family's city house had a pipe system. Piped water would have been a status symbol, though a dangerous one, in the way a diet high in red meat meant you had money, and also that you might develop heart disease. But the most plausible explanation for the lead overdose was that John and Isaac had ingested it with their food.

Archaeologist Joseph B. Lambert, in his 1997 book *Traces of the Past,* described the use of lead by Josiah Wedgwood, the English potter. Wedgwood had attempted to imitate Chinese porcelain, copying the "oriental" style in plates that he could sell in England. The imitations were cream-colored and lacquered with a clear lead glaze, which differed from the salt glazes and tin glazes then in common use. It's likely that the families who collected the hair used this fashionable "china." The family would have scraped the dregs of duck and juice from their plates, and here was a possible source of the lead poisoning.

One study that looked at lead levels in the bones of former slaves seemed to support this guess. At Clifts plantation, in Westmoreland County, Virginia, a pathologist named Arthur Aufderheide dug up graves and tested two sets of skeletons, those belonging to five tobacco planters (the slave owners), another group from eleven enslaved workers (an invasive profession, archaeology, with its nonchalant exhumations; as voyeuristic as ancient DNA analysis). The average lead content of the planters' skeletons was 185 parts per million (within a range of 128–258 ppm); whereas the bones of the enslaved had an average level of 35 ppm (within a range of 8–96 ppm). The researcher pointed out that an American at the end of the twentieth century might have 50 ppm lead in his or her bone.

It would be too much to say that John Ball died at age twenty-six from lead ingestion, but the possibility can't be excluded. Records show that families of some of the hair samples experienced occasional and mysterious "death clusters." One couple, an aunt and uncle of William Ball, had twelve children between 1833 and 1858; but these parents saw nine of their children die before the age of ten. Then, at the age of forty-two, the mother died. Had there been an inadvertent poisoning? At various times, family members experienced rampant malaria, gout, chronic fatigue, diabetes, and other illnesses. Not all of this can be blamed on crude medical care.

The world paid attention to toxins after the Minimata Bay disaster. In the 1950s, Minimata, a town on Japan's eastern shore, seemed to have more than its share of children with neurological and developmental defects, as well as large numbers of adults with muscle dysfunction. It was found that a chemical plant had been discharging mercury-saturated waste into Minimata Bay. People ate fish from the bay, and the resulting methylmercury poisoning led to forty deaths and hundreds of severe deformities among children born to poisoned women. Another mercury disaster occurred in 1972, this time in Iraq. Mercury-treated wheat seeds, intended for planting (mercury saturation had supposedly made them resistant to fungus), had instead been ground into flour and baked. Contamination affected thousands and more than 500 died.

John Ball's mercury levels weren't too bad, 3.3 µg, just under the mean, which meant that perhaps he wasn't receiving mercury as medicine. (His nephew Isaac Ball showed a result of more than three times the norm, so it's possible he'd had a recent fever treated with mercury.) Many doctors dispensed mercury against all sorts of illness. Neither did John have much strontium in his body, about 3 µg, a bit more than his nephew, but less than the mean. But John Ball's hair returned high concentrations of arsenic, as had his nephew's. Against a mean of 1.1 µg of arsenic, John was carrying 3.3 µg, or three times the norm (Isaac Ball showed 5.12 µg, 4.65 the mean).

A 2004 study looked at chronic disease in adults exposed to arsenic-contaminated drinking water. It happens that inorganic arsenic appears in much groundwater, as material dissolved from rock (inorganic arsenite and arsenate); and also as organic arsenic from metabolism, primarily from plants and bacteria. The study (at the University of South Carolina) investigated the correlation between high arsenic exposure and several chronic diseases, and argued that long-term exposure was associated with depression, high blood pressure, and circulatory problems.

IT SHOULD BE SAID that the *Journal of the American Medical Association* has criticized commercial hair test labs, such as the ones that looked at John's and Isaac's samples. In 2001, a researcher for that journal sent hair cuttings from a single individual to nine labs and found that toxic analysis gave widely different results, while the labs had conflicting references for normal mineral content. Trace Elements and Doctor's Data, the two labs that looked at the hair samples, gave normal arsenic levels of less than 1 and less than 0.60 per million, respectively.

Maybe hair mineral analysis is a dubious science. Or perhaps the toxins had come from the air. (In the rooms where the hair was stored, a lot of people smoked and burned coal, two sources of lead and arsenic.) One person who won't know is John Ball, the little mama's boy, who died in his twenties, of an indiscernible cause.

10 *Faith in Fathers*

JEFF BALL IS a cousin of mine who lives in South Carolina, where he works for a suburban town inspecting new construction for code and zoning. He's married a second time and has children from both events. Jeff's grandfather and mine had been brothers, two sons of Isaac Ball, the war veteran who'd written poetry. Jeff has a sharp resemblance to Isaac, whose photograph from 1870 or thereabouts shows a chin, eyes, and cheeks much like those on my cousin. Isaac and his wife, Mary Louisa, had had twelve children, or so it's been said; DNA screens had given familiar family truths a provisional tremble. With Native American markers on hand, and with the enigma of Kate Fuller, standard facts seemed more like hypotheses.

My father and Jeff's father had been first cousins, which

placed Jeff and me in the jackknife configuration of first cousins, once removed. Five marriages and large numbers of sex acts stood between us, creating a sizable genetic distance. I went in search of a paternity lab.

IT'S THE MOST tearful zone of DNA science, the one in which a buccal swab can tell you who was in the bedroom at the moment of conception. The field's untouching and crass label is the "parentage market." Clients of parentage testing range from suspicious husbands, to pregnant mistresses, to family courts stalking dads for child support. Cases end in melodrama. "You're the father!" is one denouement. "You're not the father!" another.

Vita-Med is a big DNA and blood lab in the Toronto suburbs, where it fills a two-story, supermarket-sized brick building in a light industrial neighborhood ten miles from downtown. When I visited, security felt a notch above corporate norms, a swipe card opening the door from reception, another swipe to inner chambers. Wide halls, gleaming floors, the lab itself behind a glass wall. White coats, latex gloves, test tubes.

The lab director of Vita-Med, Roxanne Chan, is a compact woman of about forty who cuts her shining black hair in a Mod style, to the collar in the back, bangs in the front. She speaks fluid, accented English. Chan wears a conservative black skirt and black tights, a cable-knit pink sweater over a pink shirt, and a finish of pink lipstick. The pink is the concession; she has no jewelry.

She leads the way to the main lab, a room close to a tennis court in square footage, with low ceilings and long tables. Centrifuges, refrigerators, computers, shelves with Petri dishes, bottles, tubes, and pipettes abound. There are biohazard signs on cabinets and twenty people at stations, except when they push back, careening on wheeled chairs.

Vita-Med does paternity tests for American courts, many of them in family justice, with each court processing hundreds of cases a year. It's high volume DNA, which justifies a second, icier name for the business, the "paternity industry." The goal is to assign fatherhood in legal actions, especially child custody and child support, immigration and adoption. Roxanne Chan says the lab does most testing through the mail, anonymously, by code. But a small number of private clients are face-to-face transactions, and these cause the most trouble. Such people can have lawyers, and lab techs get nervous about the tracking numbers on their test tubes.

There's a third, striking phrase in Chan's business: the "nonpaternity event." Nonpaternity is said to occur when the father of record (on the birth certificate) is not the child's biological father, because the mother has gotten pregnant by someone else. Geneticists estimate that between 3 and 5 percent of children are unbeknownst nonpaternal births. If this is true (and the estimate sounds high), it would amount, in the United States, to 200,000 babies each year whose parents are misrecorded.

When the news goes out by registered mail that a client isn't the father of his child, Chan says, her phone usually rings the next day. She shakes her head. Science credentials haven't helped with explosive outcomes. "They didn't teach me anger management in graduate school," she says. "But I've learned a trick. You hold the phone three feet from your ear while they scream, so you don't get hearing damage."

Vita-Med sent two cheek swab collection kits, which my cousin Jeff and I returned by mail. If everyone had been faithful, the results would show that we possessed the same Y chromosome. If we did not, then something had gone badly in someone's marriage.

THE Y CHROMOSOME has collected followers, a set of specialists in its behavior. An authority on a single chromosome is a bit like a curator in a museum; he advocates for and guards a single area of genetic material. Mark Jobling is a Y-chromosome spokesman, a geneticist who doesn't care much for the gene set other than the male-defining Y. Jobling is British, tall, thin, fortyish, and long-nosed, with a buzz-cut hairstyle and working man's accent. He wears blue jeans and a plaid shirt under a rust-colored sweater. There is nothing macho about his speech, however, which is gentle to the point of retiring. He moves his arms a little when he talks, palms out, but unemphatically.

There's snow and slush at the University of Leicester, in central England. Dark has fallen, although it is only about 4:30 in the afternoon. Mark Jobling sits in his office in a white 1960-something building. Behind him, the file cabinets have taped-up signs: "Sex chromosomes" and "Y polymorphism." Outside his door, the familiar lab with its shelved tables, DNA sequencers, and centrifuges. (Downstairs, coincidentally, is Jobling's colleague Alec Jeffreys, who has already turned up in these pages.)

Mark Jobling took a degree in biochemistry, then a PhD, both at Oxford. He dates his attraction to the Y chromosome to his doctorate. "We were interested at the time, as many people were, in the sex-determining gene, which hadn't yet been isolated," Jobling says. After that gene appeared, in 1990, Jobling stayed on good terms with the Y, and he has never left it.

Jobling's recent research involves the interaction of surnames with the male sex chromosome. In a large surname study, Jobling had asked the question, Do unrelated men who carry the same surname also possess the same Y chromosome? "If you have two guys called Blogstead, you can ask whether they have a common male ancestor, if they share a haplotype or profile," he says.

Surnames in England were adopted in the fourteenth century, prior to which most people didn't have them. The question of the study had been whether a sole individual had adopted each surname (the medieval population being tiny), which would mean that most contemporary male users would carry the same Y haplotypes; or whether names had been chosen both randomly and simultaneously by many people around the country, in which case a contemporary sample of male users of the same name would show a variety of Y chromosomes.

"We looked at about forty surnames, from common ones to rare," Jobling says. "We weren't looking at families, but the reverse, at a random assortment of people. We would recruit a hundred men with a given name, spread all over the British Isles. All they shared was the name. Did they share the same Y chromosome? The short answer was yes. An example is the name Attenborough. There were two thousand people named Attenborough on the British electoral roles. Half would be men. We sampled fifty or sixty, and eighty-seven percent of men with that name turned out to have exactly the same Y haplotypes, even though they didn't know each other at all. So it seems there was a single founder, and you had other lineages coming into the group through illegitimacies, nonpaternity."

In 1997, geneticist Michael Hammer of the University of Arizona used similar methods to identify a "rabbinical haplotype." The Jewish priesthood arose about three thousand years ago, and paternal descent from a rabbi has always been the method by which male Jews enter the clergy. Hammer and two collaborators demonstrated the existence of a Y-chromosome profile common to rabbis (the Cohen modal haplotype, a name derived from the rabbinical surname, Cohen).

Jobling's surname study had involved Y-STR screening, which looked at perhaps twenty different "short tandem repeat" markers on the Y chromosome. Data from STR tests resemble random strings of numbers in which each digit refers to a specific marker. In a profile—for instance, 15, 13, 32, 25, 10, 11, 13, 11, 15, 11, 11, 10, 12, 14, 25, 22, 11, 12, 17, 23—each number represents the number of repeat units at a particular site. The first number, 15, means that at the marker called DYS19, the nucleotide figure T-A-G-A appears fifteen times. The tenth number, 11, refers to marker DYS438, where the sequence G-A-A-A-A appears eleven times.

The exception to the rule that surnames and Y chromosomes tend to travel together turns up in common family names. "If you take Smith, fifty men will have a spectrum of Y chromosomes, like the general population," says Jobling. "Not surprising, because there are five hundred and sixty thousand people called Smith in England and Wales, or one point three five percent of the population. So presumably that name was established by many individuals who took it on as an occupational name, for blacksmithing. On the other end, the study had one curiosity in the name set. One of the names we studied, a very rare one, with only one hundred and twenty-seven people using it, showed a mixture of black African and Northern European Y-chromosome types. It was a Yorkshire name, first recorded there in thirteen-seventy. We recruited twenty-seven men, all white, who thought themselves unrelated, and nine of them had a chromosome that is the most African of African Y chromosomes. Looking at African databases, there are only three of these Ys in the literature. One is Berber, from northern Africa, and two are from Mali. On the African tree, the Y-type they carried is also the oldest type it's possible to have."

Jobling hazarded an explanation for the funky data. During the sixteenth and seventeenth centuries, he said, there had been a lot of immigration of Africans to England as servants. At some point, a male servant might have fathered a son with a white woman, and her mixed-race son grew up with the "legitimate" family name. It was a scenario similar to the one I imagined for the "Indian" markers in the hair samples.

THE MALE-ACTIVATING segment of the Y chromosome is a teensy gene, a hiccup on the genome called SRY (*s*ex-determining *r*egion *Y*). It's frequently called a "switch," because the only thing it does is to turn on masculinization. SRY appears on the short arm of the Y chromosome, near its tip. One theory describes its behavior as a sort of sabotage perpetrated on the fetus. In the nucleus, the protein expressed by the SRY gene binds to other DNA in a way that distorts its shape, altering its properties and provoking the expression of otherwise-dormant, male-making genes. The idea, in sum, is that SRY must disfigure the normal course of fetal development in order to make a boy.

Jobling says the crux lies in the gonads. "It's clear that SRY is necessary and sufficient to switch on testis differentiation. As an embryo, you start off with a gonad that could go either way, become either an ovary or a testis. If there is a Y chromosome, the SRY protein is around the place, and this gonad becomes a testis."

The other steps in masculinization, such as testicle descent and formation of the genitals, involve genes that aren't on the Y chromosome. Jobling describes an experiment that showed how sex characteristics were keyed by non-Y genes. "It was a mouse made from female cells, so it didn't have a Y chromosome," Jobling says. (Males have one X and one Y chromosome: females have two Xs.) "And all that was done was to give it a small piece of DNA containing the mouse SRY gene. The embryo developed into a completely male mouse, with male testes and male behavior. The mouse turned out to be infertile, however, because you need some other genes on the Y to make sperm properly."

The human Y chromosome, which is the smallest one, averages sixty million base pairs and can be divided into several regions. A section of euchromatin runs for about twenty-five million bases. (In any chromosome, euchromatin is an uncondensed stretch in which many genes occur.) Adjoining the euchromatin is a segment of heterochromatin, condensed DNA that contains few or no genes, varying in length from a very short piece up to forty million bases. A third area of the Y is the very small (2.5 million base pair) pseudoautosomal region, which occupies the two ends of the chromosome, its tips. About fifteen genes appear here, and during recombination in male meiosis (leading to the formation of sperm), the pseudoautosomal region is the part that exchanges material with the partner chromosome to the Y, the X chromosome. (It's pseudoautosomal because it behaves "like the autosomes," in other words, mingling material, like the other twenty-two chromosome pairs.) Although the Y chromosome is sometimes described as nonrecombining, meaning that it doesn't exchange genes with a partner, these small bits of the Y do swap material in what Jobling calls the "obligate recombination event." Recombination is required, because its failure can produce sexual ambiguity in the fetus. One possible outcome is Turner syndrome, the absence of one of the two X chromosomes in women, or sometimes, XXY syndrome, in which the doubling of the X chromosome in a male prevents a boy from undergoing puberty.

During the 1990s, Jobling was approached to do some Y-related tests in the long-running Thomas Jefferson–Sally Hemings dispute. Sally Hemings, the fifty-year-old Jefferson's teenage slave, gave birth to at least five children, and during his life, Jefferson was publicly alleged to have been the father. Two centuries later, the idea dawned to test the Y chromosomes of Jefferson and Hemings descendants. "We were sent DNA samples which were coded, so we didn't know who was who," Jobling said. (Two other geneticists were involved, Chris Tyler-Smith, at Oxford, and Peter de Knijff, in Leyden, the Netherlands.) Of Sally Hemings's male children, Eston Hemings was the only one for whom a patrilineal descendant could be traced. Thomas Jefferson had no direct (white) male descendants, so for the Jefferson Y chromosome, samples came from five descendants of Thomas's paternal uncle, Field Jefferson. Another group of samples came from descendants of two of Jefferson's nephews.

"A problem for the Jefferson family when he was alive was that Sally Hemings's children looked like Thomas, and everyone said that was the case," Jobling says. "So to explain that, Jefferson's granddaughter alleged that one of his nephews, whose surname was Carr, had been the father of Sally's children. Ultimately, the Carr descendants had a completely different type of Y chromosome, not seen in any other samples. But Eston Hemings's descendants had the same Y chromosomes as Field Jefferson's descendants. One interpretation of that was that Eston was the son of Thomas Jefferson. That's supported by the fact that the chromosome type was extremely rare. Had it been common, we couldn't have set much store on the results. The problem remains that it could have been Thomas Jefferson's brother, Randolph, or another paternal relation. Because Randolph wasn't a big name, we don't know as much about his movements. But it has been shown by documentary records that

Thomas Jefferson and Sally Hemings were at Monticello nine months before the birth of every one of her children, so it's a prima facie case. It seems to me that it's quite likely he was the father of Eston, and possibly the other children."

Jobling walks the lab, pointing out the familiar refrigerators, pipettes, and DNA sequencers ("the machines are boring, but expensive"). A pair of black machines the size of toasters sit alone on a table. "The PCR machines," he says.

I asked whether Jobling had ever met Kary Mullis, creator of PCR. Jobling laughs for the first time, and says, "I've heard about him. I heard he was supposed to have dreamed up PCR while under the influence of a large spliff. Or something like that."

RAPE INVESTIGATORS are the main users of Y-profiling tests. A physical exam after a rape might recover swabs from a woman's vagina, but semen and vaginal fluid are mingled: a Y-STR test is used because it amplifies only the rapist's DNA. Commercial Y-STR kits, marketed to police departments, have macho brand names, like PowerPlex Y and Y-filer, that in context sound inappropriate, the bad choices of marketing.

As elsewhere in the genome, markers on the Y chromosome each have a name or number. Most names for Y markers include the prefix "DYS" (for *D*NA *Y* chromosome *s*egment), as in DYS390, meaning Y marker 390. In 1999, forensic examiners settled on a common Y-chromosome profile, or "minimal haplotype," with which to build databases. It consisted of nine short tandem repeat markers

(DYS19, DYS385I, DYS385II, DYS389I, DYS389II, DYS390, DYS391, DYS392, and DYS393), a group later increased to eleven markers and labeled the "U.S. extended haplotype." A single reaction called multiplex PCR amplifies all the markers simultaneously, and the results are digested by frequency estimates, equations that guess the number of occurrences of the profile in a population.

The drama that DNA brings to the courtroom depends on these obscure formulas, which forensics borrows from population studies. Equations differ for Y-chromosome evidence and for non-Y profiles, but in both cases they're hard to describe to jurors, who might see them as academic gibberish. In 1997, the National Academy of Sciences issued recommendations for estimating random match probabilities, an arcane subject with high stakes, since a scripted presentation of numbers at the right moment in a trial can throw a capital verdict. The scene has two standard moments. First, the forensic witness makes a statement about the evidence, such as, "The sample DNA matches the suspect's DNA at the thirteen marker sites examined." The prosecutor follows this meek observation with a stunning statistic on match probability, the likelihood that a random person would possess the same profile as that of the sample, like, "The chance of a random match is fifty-seven billion to one." End of scene and movie.

MY COUSIN JEFF BALL and I had submitted cheek swabs to Vita-Med, in a search for nonpaternity in the family of one of the hair samples. The Y-STR test results came back.

They implied you could stack the two Y chromosomes on top of each other and not know the difference. A table showed their sameness. As against the U.S. extended haplotype, Vita-Med used a set of ten markers.

DNA MARKER	Sample #1	Sample #2
DYS391	10	10
DYS389I	13	13
DYS439	11	11
DYS389II	33	33
DYS438	11	11
DYS392	11	11
DYS393	13	13
DYS390	25	25
DYS385I	11	11
DYS385II	15	15

The two profiles were identical—which meant no evidence of nonpaternity, and relief, mixed with disappointment.

POLICE DEPARTMENTS have put the Y chromosome to work, and so have anthropologists. At universities, a (father-related) Y-centered field of history—better, of prehistory, the story of humans before writing—runs alongside the (mother-related) mitochondrial DNA-centered storytelling that led to the out-of-Africa model. Just as mitochondrial haplotypes show ancestral origin (the alleged Native American stamp on William Ball), Y-STR profiles also suggest geographic roots.

The data lie scattered across public and private computer servers. Humboldt University, in Berlin, maintains the biggest Y-related information set, where a nonprofit called the International Forensic Y-User Group, an affiliation of Y-chromosome labs, keeps male genetic profiles at Humboldt's molecular biology department. In 2007, the database contained more than 50,000 DNA profiles, representing several hundred populations. Partner labs send blocks of new data, and the number swells. The Mormon Church, the FBI, and various corporations that sell Y-STR tests run other Y databases. But profile sets can be small. A screening might take in a hundred men in northern Greece plus fifty or sixty in Buenos Aires, Seoul, or Algiers. This is like using a hand-drawn map that shows how to drive from Boston to New York—most of the roads don't appear. Nevertheless, forensics makes use of such databases to say where a perpetrator (or victim) might have come from. Historians make use of them to point at deep history, people and events thousands of years ago.

The Y-STR profile that Vita-Med had returned allowed me to mine some of the data. Based on Mark Jobling's surname conclusion, that names and Y-types travel together, and based on the all-clear nonpaternity results of a single test, I made the wishful assumption that my profile would have been shared by all the men named Ball among the hair samples, had there been a way to test them. In other words, Jeff Ball's and my Y chromosome was "the" Ball family Y. From several databases, I uncovered pieces of the story of this particular chromosome type.

The Ball family Y seemed to settle into a haplogroup

called *R1a,* which turns out to be a rare set. Only about 4 percent of European and white American men carry R1a markers. A genealogy Web site in the United States offered a bit of pseudo-history, combining evidence and speculation.

> The R1a lineage is believed to have originated in the Eurasian Steppes north of the Black and Caspian Seas. This lineage may have appeared in a population of the Kurgan culture, known for the domestication of the horse (approximately 3000 B.C.E.). These people are also said to have been the first speakers of the Indo-European language group. The lineage is currently found in central and western Asia, India, and in Slavic populations of Eastern Europe, and is less common in Western Europe.

In other words, the family's Y might not be "Nordic" at all. It wasn't English or French, but originated in southeastern Europe, a region that became one homeland of the Slavs.

A couple of Web sites in England gave more specifics, or conjectures. (The research didn't inspire confidence, but I took a liking to it, because it had nice romantic touches.) The male founder(s) of the R1a haplogroup apparently lived 15,000 years ago, among a group of humans huddling against an ice bank in the foothills of the Ural Mountains. During the last Ice Age, which lasted from about 20,000 to 10,000 BCE, glaciers crept down from the north and covered the upper half of Europe, from the Pyrenees in the west over to the Black Sea in the east. The human population, which had already been resident on the continent for tens of thousands of years, was forced to retreat to the south. Human settlements withdrew from the ice into three separate enclaves: one pocket of society in present-day Spain, a second in an area just north of the Balkans, and a third in what is central Ukraine. In the easternmost or "Ukrainian" colony—which from speculative maps looks as though it stood right against the ice shelf—a mutation took place in the Y that created the R1a haplogroup. When the ice retreated (over a period of a thousand years), the three colonies came out of isolation to repopulate Europe.

I was now in a position to revise the family origins narrative that I'd learned as a child. Instead of the son of a yeoman farmer who had come to America from England to remake himself into a plantation lord, I imagined our family founder to have been a bearskin-covered brute scrounging against an endless cold. He was a man who had no writing and no government, though he perhaps had a hut, and maybe the outlines of a society. A distinguished family patriarch who might have spoken a proto-language and engaged in cave painting with charcoal. In other words, the family had been founded by a man from whom a bourgeois American would run in fear.

11 *Machines for the Molecule*

THE POLYMERASE chain reaction takes a noiseless, shoebox-size machine about an hour to complete. Open the lid, add a speck of DNA, close and start. Come back when the cycle is done, and remove a billion times the amount of DNA that went in. The most important process in DNA science, and it reminds you of laundry (although you rarely take more clothes out of the wash than you load). The polymerase chain reaction has remade a dozen fields, from archaeology (old bones), to forensics (law enforcement), medicine (disease-linked genes and pharmacogenetics), agriculture (genetic modification of food), family law (the paternity industry), and genetics (the Human Genome Project and DNA databases).

DNA is too small to evaluate in numbers of one, five hundred, or even five hundred thousand molecules. The sequencing machines that read off the nucleotides work best with millions of copies of a molecular segment. Prior to the polymerase chain reaction (PCR), which spread around the world in the late 1980s, the copying method for DNA involved bacteria. One planted genetic sequences in a bacterium or yeast and waited a few days while the organism duplicated the implant. Feasible, but tedious and unpredictable. PCR accelerated the process, the bullet replacing the catapult.

It's hard to describe PCR without using The Vocabulary, especially since the polymerase chain reaction is itself a hinge term. But an ancient DNA specialist I met had an analogy.

Suppose you have a copy of the Bible, which you cut up into individual pages and throw on the floor. The mess is like a DNA sample. Suppose that page 337 is important, and you want to pull it up for examination. It would be a fluke to rustle around on the floor and come up with the right sheet of paper. However, if you make a million copies of page 337 before throwing the dismembered Bible on the floor, it becomes much easier to pick out a copy of the needed sheet. The polymerase chain reaction works in this way, much like a photocopier for genes. PCR takes an enzyme, called DNA polymerase, which is made by bacteria and is the copying machine. And it takes what are called primers, molecular fragments that tell the enzyme where to start and stop copying on the DNA molecule. If you want page 337, the primers instruct the reaction to start copying on page 336 and stop on page 338. Combine polymerase and primer, put in the piece of DNA you want to duplicate, add nucleotides (the copying toner), and you end up with a big stack of page 337, the desired section of DNA.

Polymerase. A group of enzymes called polymerases, known since the 1950s, manipulate nucleic acids. Encountering a single strand of DNA, DNA polymerases take guanine, cytosine, thymine, and adenine, and match them to their complements, synthesizing whole, double-stranded DNA.

Chain reaction. A repetitive reaction is built into the double-helix design. When a cell divides, DNA unzips into two strands, and free nucleotides attach to each strand, making two double-stranded molecules. PCR causes this process to recur over and over, in a chain reaction. The duplicate DNA makes duplicates, and the number of identical copies rises exponentially.

PCR involves four components: a DNA target sequence (the forensic bit from the crime scene); primers (short, single-stranded DNA); nucleotides (G, A, C, and T, unattached); and the enzyme that carries out the reaction, DNA polymerase. The enzyme is typically one called *Taq* polymerase, chosen for its equanimity in hot conditions. PCR uses cycles of heat to extend its copying work, and most enzymes stop working at high temperatures, except for *Taq* polymerase, which does well in scalding heat. (*Taq*, pronounced "tack," is short for *Thermus aquaticus*; the enzyme was first isolated from a bacterium of that name that lives in the hot springs of Yellowstone National Park.)

In forensics, the first stage of sample analysis involves PCR. Suppose an investigator wants to know the race of the suspect. One way to find out would be to examine hypervariable sequence 1 of a mitochondrial DNA sample, starting at base 16,039 and continuing for 325 bases. The 325-base-pair segment would be the target sequence, the place where (in this case) certain nucleotide variations suggest (maternal) ancestry. Primers, the second component of PCR, "find" this target. If a 325-base-pair section of DNA resembles a ladder with 325 rungs, a primer looks like just one side of a short section of the ladder, a half-ladder, with a rail and only twenty half-rungs. Since the 1970s, primers have been made by automation, synthesized to match a single strand of target DNA at a place where a few base pairs complement it. PCR uses two primers to copy the target. One attaches to the "left" end of the target, down toward the bottom of the strand, the other to the "right" side of the target, near the top. These two primers define the beginning and the end of the segment to be duplicated. Nucleotides, the third ingredient in PCR, are the rump bits in solution: guanine, adenine, cytosine, and thymine. And polymerase, the fourth, guides the nucleotides into place to attach where they belong.

PCR machines, called thermocyclers because they heat and cool, take up very little room in a lab. Test tubes the size of a pinky finger go into them (racks of tubes allow many samples to be processed simultaneously), along with target DNA, primers, nucleotides, and *Taq* polymerase. The thermocycler applies heat (94°C for a minute), causing the DNA sample to separate (or "denature") into two strands.

Things cool to 60°C for a minute. The primers then attach themselves to the single strands (they "anneal") at specific places, resulting in two molecules with long, single-stranded tails but heads made of tiny double helices (the primers attached to their complementary sequences on the target DNA). The thermocycler then heats to 72°C for a minute, and the *Taq* polymerase "extends the primer." Free nucleotides anneal with the single-stranded tails. The cycle is repeated. Heat causes the two new molecules to denature. Primers attach themselves to what are now four strands. Nucleotides extend, resulting in four double-helix molecules.

After four cycles of heating and cooling, you have eight copies of the target DNA. After sixteen cycles, there are 65,476 copies, and after thirty cycles, you have 1,072,758,784 identical segments. Some of this material can be loaded into a sequencer, which (in the example of the race question) reads off the arrangement of the 325 mtDNA bases. A piece of profiling software compares the sequence to the FBI's CODIS database, and predicts ethnicity.

One of the early biotechnology firms, Cetus Corporation, in Berkeley, patented PCR in the 1980s, and in 1991 sold it to the Switzerland-based multinational Hoffman-LaRoche for $300 million. The creator of the process, Kary Mullis, was a chemist at Cetus when he devised PCR (but gone from the company by the time of the sale). Mullis described his first imagining of PCR in his 1998 memoir, *Dancing Naked in the Mind Field.*

> Natural DNA is a tractless coil, like an unwound and tangled audio tape on the floor of the car in the dark. What kind of chemical program would be required to "FIND" a specific sequence on DNA with 3 billion nucleotides and then display that sequence to a human who was trillions of times larger than the DNA? . . . I would use a short piece [of DNA] to narrow the search. . . . It would scan over the thousand possibilities out of the first search to find just the one I wanted. And using the natural properties of DNA to replicate itself under certain conditions that I could provide, I could make that sequence of DNA between the sites where the two short search strings landed reproduce the hell out of itself . . . Not only could I make a zillion copies, but they would always be the same size. That was important. That was the almighty, the halleluja! clincher. I had just solved the two major problems in DNA chemistry. Abundance and distinction. And I had done it in one stroke.

One appealing thing about this description is that its author feels something and wants you to know it. Science presumes to be modest, emotionless, and it tends to the passive voice on the premise that data alone should speak, and investigators should have no feelings in the matter. Serious science expunges the word *I*.

Kary Mullis doesn't fit into the professional uniform of "scientist." The cover of *Dancing Naked in the Mind Field* shows the author holding a surfboard, the ocean in sunset behind him. He's bare-chested, with a wet suit from the waist down and a sly smile. The inventor of PCR sends out cowboy signals. The reader wonders, Has he retired to the beach on the money from his invention?

In fact, no. As an employee, Mullis received a thank-you letter and a bonus of $10,000 for his creation.

KARY MULLIS IS about sixty, square-jawed, with blond hair disappeared to show most of his scalp, and pretty blue eyes. You can see he'd been a vigorous man, his black T-shirt over a strong chest, and that youthfulness had only recently left his face. The man who'd posed with a surfboard was physically convincing as a beach walker. I'd expected a grandstanding person, because press and rumors had been harsh on the inventor of PCR. But he's shy and self-conscious, and seems to want to escape the attention. He's got a soft voice, no bluster, khaki pants, and loafers.

"What I am is a loner kind of thinker," he says. "I just put myself in a discovery position, and hope. And I don't know how it works. What I really like to do is read and think and write. I never thought of anything interesting in a lab. In a lab you learn what the problems are. You need to be acquainted with that. But I don't think when I'm around other people and telephones. The business of a university or private lab, there's a lot of distraction that's really worthless. But just keep immersing yourself in something, and you might get lucky."

I'd met DNA handlers who'd been flanked by assistants, labs, equipment, offices, and titles. Mullis was alone with a glass of iced tea at his dining table. The loneliness of the solo runner. It didn't seem like a mask: during a half day, the phone rang once, and it was Mullis's wife.

"I hate the phone," he says, putting it down. "I prefer it if someone walks by and comes in, unannounced."

Newport Beach, California, sixty miles south of Los Angeles, is an anonymous resort town, dotted with spas, with a marina and a palm-lined boulevard. It's surprising Kary Mullis lives here, where a fingernail salon probably replaced the last bookstore a decade ago. But the ocean is close to the door. Home for Mullis is a 1970s compound of two-story apartment buildings on a boatyard. About ten units per building, and ten buildings (stucco, tan) jigsawed together, their backs against canals and slips, with landscaping in the gaps. The apartment is a big one-bedroom, the neighbors just beyond the wall, with shared parking out in the lot.

Mullis disappears and returns with a plastic model of a molecule, one-inch balls snapped together into a foot-long snake. It's his response to the question, "What are you doing now?"

"This part here is called the alpha-gal epitope," he says, pointing at a clump of plastic atoms, without eye contact. "Humans, chimpanzees, and orangutans about twenty-five million years ago, when we were all the same thing, stopped making a connecting bond within it. Now about one percent of our immunoglobins are anti-alpha-gal antibodies. Which results in hyperacute rejection of tissue transplants from animals, such as the pig valves they put in hearts."

Alpha-gal is a sugar (alpha-galactose) that the human immune system attacks; an epitope is a piece of a molecule that the immune response specifically targets. Most animal cells carry alpha-gal on their surface, but humans lost the enzyme that sticks the sugar to the cell, so that immunoglobins treat cells that carry it as foreign, and attack them. The result is that tissue transplants from animals, so-called xenotransplants, are usually destroyed in a few minutes.

"I'm setting up a kind of virtual laboratory in different places—Georgia, Texas, Kentucky—to take this thing that antibodies attack and stick it to something that is intentionally made to bind to some pathogen that we're being bothered by now. For instance, if you'd just gotten infected with anthrax, it would be to your advantage to divert the antibodies that normally were made to get alpha-gal, to transform a percentage of those into anti-anthrax antibodies. And it seems to work. We haven't done it with anthrax, but with rats, we've diverted some antibodies to attack *Haemophilus influenza*."

The project was a business venture. Had he modestly named the company after himself? "No." Smile and eye contact, relaxation. "The company is just me and Nancy."

Nancy Cosgrove Mullis occasionally walks through. She's tall, handsome, thin, long dark hair, commanding. This is Kary Mullis's fourth marriage. Previous spouses had resulted in two sons and one daughter, all grown. Nancy Mullis is protective of her husband, who she thinks had been treated badly, "because he has a wild past." It's a reference to his years at the University of California, Berkeley, during the 1960s, and to his early jobs, when Mullis was a chemist for hire who liked to enjoy himself away from the lab. "He's the most brilliant person, the most wide-angle, well-rounded person and he needs to be listened to and respected," she says. Mullis keeps his eyes down during the praise.

I ASK MULLIS about the National Inventors Hall of Fame, the club of discoverers to which he belongs, along with Alec Jeffreys, creator of DNA fingerprinting. His eyes widen, and he says, "Another member of that group is John Bardeen!" Kary Mullis is tired of talking about the polymerase chain reaction, which changed his life, as well as that of 10,000 DNA handlers, and probably 100,000 felons, and counting, and is currently changing medicine. He prefers to talk about his own heroes.

"Five miles from here there is probably a PCR machine, but in the same radius there are probably a million transistors," he says. "John Bardeen was the inventor of the transistor, and I've talked on the phone to him! I just called him, the guy that invented the transistor! He's dead now, John Bardeen. But I was reading about him, and it said he'd retired to Carbondale, Illinois, and I called information, and there he was. I talked to him for a couple of hours, without ever saying who I was, or why I wanted to talk to him. I knew all about him and what he'd gone through. If I hadn't known about it, he certainly would have gotten rid of me. The transistor! All the people in materials physics said, you can't make a three-element solid-state device, because you can't take three different solids and put them together in a way so that they have a finite connection. A vacuum tube has a screen in the middle of a vacuum, and electrons are going through that screen, and they're hitting the cathode or not, and the charge on that screen determines how fast the flow is. Try to make something like that out of a solid. They had a diode made out of solids. But to have a thing like that out of three solids seemed impossible. Bardeen kept working at it, and he got it. It wasn't easy to manufacture, so another guy named William Shockley came up with a manufacturing process, and Bardeen and Shockley got the Nobel Prize."

"Did you identify yourself to Bardeen as a Nobel laureate?"

"No. I asked what it was like to be surrounded by millions of transistors. I asked him what he thought transistors would be used for, and he said, 'I thought they'd use them for hearing aids.' He was from the generation that listened to the radio sitting down, in the living room. It was a scream talking to him. I thought to myself, 'You're talking to the man who invented the transistor!' I think of myself as a hero every now and then, because I open *Nature* magazine and see an ad for PCR. But think of the guy who invented the transistor. That was a hero."

For Mullis, inventing PCR must have been a bit like inventing the transistor in order to improve hearing aids. In his memoir, Mullis said he'd been encouraged to devise PCR because he was tired of the slowness of making oligonucleotides, chunks of DNA, a drudgery of his job in the early 1980s at Cetus Corporation.

As an invention, PCR is a hard-to-characterize advance. It wasn't a new paradigm, like relativity; neither was it the uncovering of a life-extending substance, like penicillin. PCR is merely a tool, but it's one of shocking power.

In some ways, it's comparable to the first movie cameras. Around the year 1910, sprocket-driven motion picture cameras had launched an industry, and after 1990, PCR did the same. (To be fair, it's multiplied the commercial value of several pre-existing industries by about a thousandfold.) In 1895, when the brothers Louis and Auguste Lumière built the *cinématographe*, the first movie camera, they didn't predict that within a short time, corporations and film studios would rise on the cornerstone of their invention. Nor did they expect that fifteen years after they'd established the visual revolution, they would be pushed out of it, their role usurped by smarter businesspeople, and that they'd return to what they'd done before the movie camera, which was selling photographic plates. Some of the same things have happened to PCR, and Kary Mullis. A decade after inventing PCR, which, to repeat, was sold by his former employer for $300 million, he was again a solitary chemist, and again trying to make a living.

KARY BANKS MULLIS was born in Lenoir, North Carolina, in 1944 and moved with his family to Columbia, South Carolina, soon after. He grew up in that city, the thinly populated capital of an old-fashioned, poor state, in the 1950s.

South Carolina was not known as a place that encouraged new strands of thought. "But there were those of us who were interested in making rockets and launching frogs into space, and stuff, and nobody cared," Mullis says. "It wasn't that people were seeking you out as a nonconformist. But they weren't actively trying to stop you, either.

In fact, back then you could buy dynamite fuses at a hardware store. A thirteen-year-old boy could walk in and buy a 100-foot length of quarter-inch dynamite fuse, and they would sell it to you, and they would make a joke, like, 'What are you going to do, blow up the bank?' The drugstore up the street bought potassium nitrate in pound quantities for me. They usually had it in little bottles, and I asked the guy to get it for me in large quantities, and he did. Whereas today, somebody would say, 'I can't sell it to you, because my insurance.' I had a friend whose father had a machine shop where they had a welder, and that guy didn't mind welding fins onto a metal tube—those were our rockets and their wings. These days, the guy would say, 'No, our insurance will not allow that.' Plus, we would go out to a sand pit—somebody owned it, I'm sure, but it wasn't used any more. These days, again, people wouldn't let you. Our rockets were going up a couple of miles high. Columbia wasn't friendly to us in the sense that people were congratulating you, saying, 'Wow, you put a frog up two miles and got him back alive!' But nobody was stopping us from doing it. Sometimes the rockets would come down in the woods, and set them on fire, and we'd have to go put it out. These days, you'd attract the FBI. Chemistry was considered an odd little subject that some geeks were doing, but it wasn't dangerous. We'd put frogs up in the air. These little frogs in our yard, they would fit in a canister you used to be able to get thirty-five millimeter film in, little screw-top metal cans that could fit into the top of a rocket, with a whole bunch of padding that would protect the frog from the heat and thrust of the rocket. The frog cockpit also had to be blown out along with the nose cone and a parachute to get him back down. The rocket part would fall down by itself. The frog would fit in there, and I'm sure they hated it, because the acceleration was immense. By the time we were finished, we had rockets four feet tall, made from an alloy of aluminum and steel that was strong, but light. The whole process, if you drew a design of it for somebody, was pretty hairy. It was a pretty good design. If you wanted to go past the speed of sound, you had to have a particular nozzle called a de Laval nozzle, a tube shaped like an hourglass. You could make it out of a mixture of asbestos and plaster of Paris. One time, one of our rockets blew up as it took off. I didn't think it had the capability to blow up. It was the biggest we'd made, and I never made a big one like that again. Anyway, we lived in Columbia, four boys in the family. A two-story house with two dormers."

Mullis is walking on his balcony. Potted plants obstruct most of the floor—ferns, succulents, a few orchids. The balcony overlooks a narrow canal that leads out to a marina, and a boat putters through. Rockets launched by teenaged boys in empty gravel pits seems remote.

"I went to Georgia Tech for undergraduate, which was sensible for a kid from South Carolina, Georgia being next state over, and I got a degree in chemistry. Then came time for grad school. I'd been thinking about going to graduate school at Duke, in North Carolina, but this lady married to a friend of mine, who went out to parties with us—I'd gotten married—this woman who went out with us, her name was Beth, she said, 'Kary, you know how people won't talk to you about the things you want to talk about?' She was talking about cosmology, philosophical stuff, which interested me but didn't go over well with some other people. She said, 'At Berkeley, they would talk about it. That's what they talk about all the time.' I went to Berkeley to do a chemistry PhD, and she was absolutely right. Moving from Georgia Tech to Berkeley was like moving from Earth to Mars, except for the language being the same. I stepped right into it. I liked the whole thing. At Berkeley, there were a lot of different customs, psychedelic drugs, and free love. And that appealed to me. But I was married."

"Did you learn how to purify LSD?"

Mullis started a technical explanation. "The best way to do it is with a silica gel column—"

It was the beginning of one of the memories he had of 1960s Berkeley, where tens of thousands of people had used psychedelic drugs, and hundreds had manufactured them. In 1966, when Mullis was enrolled in the chemistry department, LSD was not yet an illegal substance, and government grants supported research into psychedelics. Mullis stops talking.

"Nancy's right, my wife is right," he says. "I can't talk about that. It has cost me dearly to be open about it. Most people aren't open about what they did then. So if you are, you stand out. I'm surprised that people use it against me, but they have, and they do."

OF THE TWO DNA household names, James Watson and Francis Crick, Mullis prefers the latter. He personally remembered Crick.

"Francis Crick used to live up the street from me when I lived in La Jolla. I saw a lot of him then, because I would go up and have dinner at his house. He would invite some of the strangest people, because he was a curious person, a real wide-angled person. I knew when I went there for dinner there would be some weirdo that would be fun to talk to. Francis tolerated and encouraged people with odd ideas, and I liked that about him. To me they weren't weirdos, actually, but they would have come across to some people as not fit company for Francis Crick. Why would he entertain psychics, for instance? He dealt with those kinds of people because there was a phenomenon to be investigated. He was interested in anything that's interesting, including cosmology, and consciousness. I think of three things together: chemistry, biology, and consciousness. There aren't boundaries in my mind between them. Talk to Francis about consciousness, you're in a heady atmosphere. He was interested in the nature of consciousness, and there's nothing more interesting than that. Most scientists don't feel comfortable with it. Most scientists don't feel comfortable with eleven-dimensional space, either. They know so little about cosmology, but they pooh-pooh it. If you say, 'This is how five-dimensional space would be. This is the sort of world, if you lived in it—this is the kind of thing that would be normal. You'd be able to walk through a wall.' They just don't see that that would be interesting. Fact is, most of those dimensions are curled up smaller than the size of a hydrogen atom, but they have an effect on things, like the gravitational field. Francis

Crick didn't care what other people thought about him, and that was very appealing."

Francis Crick died in July 2004, in San Diego, at age eighty-eight.

KARY MULLIS STARTED surfing when he was about forty-five. He hated gym machines ("I felt like a fool, pushing and pulling levers"), and one day a friend loaned him a board. "It's a great way to wake up. If you go out for an hour in the morning, the rest of the day is going to be all right." When I visited, he'd recently had surgery and taken time off from surfing. The surfboard is one of the few things people know about him, and it doesn't help, because who surfs except people with evacuated minds? Another problem, as far as gossip, is the memory of Stargene. After the success of PCR, Mullis and a friend started a company to sell the DNA of well-known people.

"I had some of Abraham Lincoln's hair, and with Stargene we wanted to provide amplified segments of various famous people's DNA," he says. "We amplified a sequence from Lincoln's hair, and confirmed it, and we said, 'We're going to make these fountain pens for Republicans who want Abraham Lincoln's DNA!' Lincoln was a Republican. Or, Elvis Presley's DNA. We weren't into it except for fun. Somebody who is an Elvis Presley fan would be thrilled to have an item, some kind of object that had in it, in a way you could never get to, so that the person who donated the DNA wouldn't have to worry about somebody doing something with the DNA in the future, for example, some of Elvis's DNA. It would be there in a form where you could say, 'That little teeny dot there is some of Elvis Presley's DNA, amplified, with his sequences in it.'"

"Did you get your hands on Elvis's DNA?"

"Unfortunately, Priscilla Presley was not interested. DNA causes strange responses in people, all sorts of irrational reactions."

WALK INTO A DNA lab, on any continent, and you confront the same beige machine. It sits near the middle of the lab, shrinelike, a cube about three feet wide and high, with computer-plastic cladding and a small glass door. The machine's presence is reassuring, like the familiar menu in a chain restaurant. Its bland exterior speaks of the offend-no-one school of design, while its insides remain mysterious, even to many of its users.

DNA science stands on two legs: the polymerase chain reaction and genetic sequencing. The beige boxes are the sequencers. After PCR cooks a segment of DNA into copious amounts, a genetic sequencer ingests this amplified soup, called the PCR product, and discerns the order of its nucleotides, identifying each of the bases in the molecule fragment. One company, Hoffman-LaRoche, controls PCR. Likewise, a single firm holds the monopoly on genetic sequencers.

Applied Biosystems Inc. (ABI) is a California-based manufacturer with about forty-five hundred employees. ABI makes 90 percent of the sequencers in use in law enforcement, drug companies, universities, hospitals, and private labs. DNA handlers complain about the lack of choice, and, like drivers and gas, they must pay.

ABI has headquarters in the San Francisco Bay area, with satellite offices on the East Coast, in Japan, the United Kingdom, and Australia. One of its divisions lies twenty miles south of San Francisco. The branch occupies an office park with not so many trees, winding streets that lead past featureless two-story buildings, and Mexican lawn crews buzzing trimmers around landscaping. It's the anonymous, lucrative face of Big Science, where a little sign at the sidewalk ("ABI") stands in inverse relationship to the scale of the operation.

Frank Stephenson, an in-house educator for the company, is a twenty-year veteran of ABI. Stephenson is about forty, with blond hair, ruddy skin, and tenor voice. He wears pleated green khakis and a white buttoned-down shirt, and he works out of a cubicle. Most ABI workers hired into accounting, sales, or maintenance don't yet speak The Vocabulary. Stephenson teaches them, running seminars on laboratories and polypeptides, DNA chemistry, and how the company's products work. He talks fast and appears tightly wound, until a disarming smile flashes.

"Kary Mullis," Stephenson says, shaking his head. "PCR is one of those inventions that everyone thinks they could have invented. Including me. Why didn't I think of that? In 1983, when Kary Mullis did think of PCR, I was working at Berkeley, and everything he had was also available to me! The template DNA, the primers, the bases, DNA polymerase—all in my laboratory! But I didn't make the connection, the little jump that he did. Therefore, he gets the Nobel Prize, and I lie awake at night, looking at the ceiling, bitter."

With that self-deprecating flourish, Stephenson walks through a big lab empty of people and into a room with four or five beige boxes.

"The most recent genetic sequencer, the 3730xl, churns out two million bases in a day," he says, pointing. He means that the bulky plastic device sitting on the table, if fully loaded and running all the time, can transcribe a DNA fragment 2 million base pairs long in twenty-four hours, spelling out its As, Cs, Ts, and Gs. Stephenson moves to another table, points at a machine four-and-a-half-feet high, two-and-a-half-feet wide and deep. "The 3700 DNA Analyzer," he says, "introduced in nineteen-ninety-five, which could sequence four hundred thousand bases a day. This is the instrument that did the Human Genome Project."

The Human Genome Project, which determined the base sequence in human DNA, began in 1990 under the auspices of the U.S. Department of Energy and the National Institutes of Health. In the United Kingdom, the Wellcome Trust became a partner, and input also came from Japan, France, Germany, and China. The project did most of its work between 1998 and 2000. At the time, Applied Biosystems (through its sister company, Celera Genomics) undertook a publicity campaign that embarrassed the federal government into a race with private industry (meaning, ABI and Celera) to complete the sequence. ABI provided 300 of its then new model 3700 sequencers to Celera, which kept them running for a year. In summer 2000, Celera, ABI, and the competing government agencies held a press conference with President Clinton in the White House to announce a "rough draft" of the genome. It was a moment of brand awareness for ABI that no biotechnology manufacturer has been able to challenge.

A GENETICIST NAMED Fred Sanger, of Cambridge University, devised the first method of DNA sequencing, "chain termination," in the 1970s. Sanger used his manual and painstaking technique to decipher the 5,386-base genetic code of the virus *Phi-X174*. The Sanger method became the standard, and among many who used it was Russell Higuchi, who deciphered a piece of quagga DNA in 1984. "Sanger determined you could sequence DNA by tricking the polymerase," Frank Stephenson says, sketching glyphs of molecular bonds on a marker board.

The Sanger method took DNA synthesis down to five component parts. They were: the genetic material to be analyzed (the sample), a second fragment that sticks to the sample (the primer), DNA polymerase (the enzyme that links nucleotides into a chain), a supply of free-floating nucleotides (bases), and another supply of modified bases, nucleotides that have been intentionally corrupted.

"A nucleotide base, like a link in a chain, has two ends," says Stephenson. "At the back end is a chemical hook called a hydroxyl group, the site where the next base attaches to continue the nucleotide chain. Fred Sanger put in nucleotides that don't have an available bond on that end of them. You could call them 'bad' bases, because they lack the hydroxyl group you need to attach the next base, the next A, C, G, or T, in replication. They're actually called dideoxynucleotide triphosphates, or ddNTPs, and they can be made, like the normal bases from which DNA is constructed. When a ddNTP gets incorporated into DNA, copying of the molecule stops right there, because nothing can be added after it. They're chain-termination bases."

Chain-terminating bases come in four varieties—the adenine, cytosine, guanine, and thymine of normal DNA—and they comprised the fifth ingredient in the soup of the Sanger method. As the replication reaction takes place, the ddNTPs are randomly selected and attached, halting the reaction at random points and yielding an output of partial copies of the sample. One fragment might read, G-A-C-T, the next one, G-A-C-T-A, a third, G-A-C-T-A-A, and a fourth, G-A-C-T-A-A-G. Sanger developed a manual method, using radioactivity, to identify the chain-terminating bases in a DNA sample and record their order, one base at a time. The Sanger method took about a day to execute and had an examination rate or "throughput" of 100 base pairs per day.

In 1982—six thousand miles west of Cambridge, in the lab of biochemist Leroy Hood at the California Institute of Technology—sequencing made a shift in emphasis. Hood attached different-colored fluorescent dyes to each of the four chain-terminators, or "bad" bases, the ddNTPs. The dyes created DNA fragments like colored flags. Hood developed a way to read them with an optical sensor that recorded their order of appearance. This allowed automation and speed-up of the handcrafted Sanger method.

Leroy Hood and partners founded Applied Biosystems with the idea to design an automated DNA sequencing machine. In 1986, using the four-color dye method, ABI produced its first DNA sequencing device.

"The 370A, it was called," says Stephenson, "which could sequence five thousand bases a day, a leap from Fred Sanger's approach, where you might get five thousand bases in two weeks. Unfortunately, we don't have any more of them." The first DNA sequencers, like most early technology, have apparently vanished. No one has them—neither customers, nor museums, nor the company that made them. They're a memory in a few photographs.

ABI based its automation of the sequencing process on a method called gel electrophoresis. Electrophoresis involves a quarter-inch-thick slab of gel the size of a sheet of legal paper. It's the consistency of Jell-O (but shaped from the synthetic material polyacrylamide) and squished between two plates of glass. At one end of the gel is an optical sensor consisting of an argon-ion laser beam, which rides back and forth like a printer head and does the actual "reading" of the DNA. Electrophoresis is a way to make molecules move through a porous medium (the gel), using an electric field. Because DNA has a negative charge, if you generate an electric field that is positive at one end of the gel and introduce the amplified DNA from PCR at the other end, the genetic material will slowly move through the medium (a distance of about a foot), toward the positive charge, where the optical element scans it.

When amplified, chain-terminated DNA comes out of the PCR machine, it has been transformed from a small sample into a huge bunch of DNA fragments. The bits range from ten to 1,000 bases long, and each piece is a gradually larger section of the original sample (G-A-C-T, G-A-C-T-A, G-A-C-T-A-A, G-A-C-T-A-A-G). Gel electrophoresis separates the pieces according to size. The sheet of polyacrylamide has grooves along its length, like rake lines made by a comb, such that many samples of amplified DNA, placed at the top of separate grooves, or lanes, can be sequenced simultaneously (twenty-four samples, forty-eight, ninety-six, depending on the machine).

In operation, the process looks a bit like microwaving. A technician places a rack of small test tubes in the sequencer. Each tube holds a different sample of amplified DNA (a crime-scene sample, a medical experiment, whatever). A robot arm selects the individual tubes and deposits their contents into receptacles at the end of one lane of the sheet of gel. The electric field begins to pull the DNA through the polyacrylamide. The smallest bits (G-A-C-T) move the fastest; behind them are the next smallest pieces (G-A-C-T-A); behind them, the next (G-A-C-T-A-A), and so on, up to the biggest piece. At the end of each fragment, there is a chain terminator base, which carries a tiny bit of fluorescent dye (blue = C, green = A, yellow = G, red = T). The fragments, after an hour or so, reach the end of the gel, where they file into a waste tray in strict order of size, smallest to largest. As they pass in this drill formation, they cross in front of the argon-ion laser, which shines on the individual fragments, makes the dye glow, and sends a record of the terminating nucleotide to a piece of software. The software then reconstructs the sequence of the DNA strand and renders a graph of the nucleotide sequence (four differently colored lines for the four bases). Alternatively, it generates the sequence in a stream of letters (G-A-C-T-A-A-G-C-C-T-A-C-T-A-A-A-G-G-G-C-T-C-T . . .). Either in graph form, or in nucleotide babble, the data are mesmerizing and incoherent, until another piece of software digests it, comparing it to existing datasets of genes or markers, and interpreting the meaning of the sequence.

Like the Sanger method, gel electrophoresis has had its season. Although some ABI machines use it, a faster replacement technology appeared in 1997 that uses thin tubes, or capillaries, in place of gelatin.

Stephenson removes a rack the size of a book from one sequencer, and the thing seems to quiver. It consists of ninety-six golden strands, each the width of a human hair and arranged in an undulating pattern, like golden tresses, trembling. They look like a shoulder-length wave, frozen in motion. "Appears to be like metal, but they're actually glass, coated with a polymer that allows them to bend without breaking," Stephenson says. "The fragments are electrophoresed through the capillaries and read by the optical unit, same as it was with the gel, only much faster."

The first DNA sequencer, in 1987, had a cycle time of about six hours and used a Hewlett-Packard Vetra computer to compile the base order. It operated with perhaps twenty kilobytes of memory ("Laughable," says Stephenson). The next generation, in 1993, used an Apple operating system, and the third generation, in 1997, went back to a Microsoft Windows standard. A fourth generation of sequencers appeared in 2004.

FRANK STEPHENSON is impatient with forensic examiners. They represent the largest market for genetic sequencers, but they're reluctant to upgrade. Police labs tend to use a slow but predictable ABI machine called the 310. "And they've done it for years," says Stephenson, shaking his head. "Scotland Yard, Royal Canadian Mounted Police, FBI. Because their machines have to be tested and retested, and most of the labs are government-run, it's hard to get anyone to change standards."

In addition to sequencers, Applied Biosystems sells PCR machines (Roche owns the patent and leases it to ABI), protein sequencers (which read amino acid arrangements), DNA synthesizers (which make primers), peptide synthesizers (which make pieces of protein), mass spectrometers (a beige box the size of a car that determines the molecular content of anything it ingests), and devices that measure gene expression—"What genes are expressed in different tissue types, from healthy cells to cancer," Stephenson says. It's an impressive command over the molecular world.

From the perspective of the lab bench, ABI's market coverage falls like a blanket, reassuring and suffocating. The company sells the refills for its sequencers—gels, DNA polymerase, nucleotides, and other solutions—and it sells maintenance contracts, with crews that fly around the world for on-site service. The monopoly is reminiscent of one formerly held by IBM, the office-machine company. In the 1960s and '70s, International Business Machines (known as Big Blue for the color of its blocky logo) looked unassailable as the leading maker of typewriters and adding machines. Its grip on office life seemed total, and its service contracts and supply of consumables promised permanent revenue and control. But with the surprise appearance of the personal computer, IBM faded. Its three-letter acronym, however dominant, was no protection.

KARY MULLIS'S OFFICE, which consists of a desk overlooking a boat canal, has some shelves with family photos, and next to them are the awards. On a glass shelf sits the Japan Prize, the highest science honor in Japan, and near it is the Nobel Prize. Both came in 1993. Both are gold medals, like big coins, two inches in diameter. The Japan Prize has a modernist, spare design, a relief in the shape of a crescent. The Nobel is more traditional, reflecting its Edwardian origins. On one side of the medal is a profile of Alfred Nobel, inventor of dynamite, industrialist, benefactor of the prize that he established in 1901. On the other is a relief depicting two women dressed in gauzy gowns who appear to be standing on a cloud. It's ethereal, a bit like a Symbolist painting.

"Some kind of Swedish mythological thing," Mullis speculates. "I don't know what it's about. What it represents to me is partially undraped women, and I thought that was pretty cool."

Mullis has nothing precious or knowing in his manner. He's open and vulnerable, and willing to feel. "I heard a story that explains why there is no Nobel Prize in math," he said. "And the reason, the folklore explanation, anyway, is that Alfred Nobel had a tragic romance with a woman who ran off with a mathematician, so that put a scourge on the whole profession."

Next to the Nobel on the shelf is a snapshot of a mushroom with a golden ocher cap and pale yellow stem. "That's my favorite mushroom, *Amanita calyptroderma*, which I collect and eat."

Kary Mullis, when he received the Nobel in Stockholm in December 1993, gave a speech. In it, he described his first unsuccessful tinkering after coming upon the idea for PCR. He said, in part:

> For three months I did sporadic experiments while my life at home and in the lab with [my girlfriend] was crumbling. It was slow going. Finally, I retreated from the idea of starting with human DNA, I wasn't even absolutely sure that the Genentech sequence from *Nature* that I was using was from a single exon. I settled on a target of more modest proportions, a short fragment from pBR322, a purified plasmid. The first successful experiment happened on December 16th. I remember the date. It was the birthday of Cynthia, my former wife from Kansas City, who had encouraged me to write fiction and bore us two fine sons. I had strayed from Cynthia eventually to spend two tumultuous years with [another woman]. When I was sad for any other reason, I would also grieve for Cynthia. There is a general place in your brain, I think, reserved for "melancholy of relationships past." It grows and prospers as life progresses, forcing you finally, against your grain, to listen to country music.

Mullis leads the way out of his apartment and down a path to the waterfront, where a hundred boats float, moored to the docks. Beyond them, a waterway, and a view to the open water. Mullis is thinking, trying to bring back a mood from melancholy.

"You can't say the world today is a whole lot better place than it was twenty years ago, that we're slowly improving it," he says. "We certainly aren't. We need some shocking new kinds of concepts to get us out of what we're in right now, which is scary to think about. That it's all tangled up with religions and races and stuff requires some heavy thinking. And I don't think anything that's catalytic to that should be thought of as bad. We're not doing fine—at all. Somebody who says, 'All we have to do is keep doing exactly what we're doing right now, and we'll be all right'—they're missing something very important. The world is not as nice or safe a place now as it was a couple of decades ago. It's much worse. A lot of things need to be rethought. I don't know what the answer is. But it's not close yourself up with one little philosophy and cling to it till you die, and you'll be all right. Scientists are for questioning everything. There are plenty of us out there, and there's plenty of time to do it."

Harriet Waring

12 *The Phantom Mutation*

An expanding file of forensic reports, and expanding ambiguity. There were two more strands of hair, but they didn't promise much. The one called "Harriet Waring" appeared in folded paper identical to that holding "Aunt Cingie," cut about 1842. She was probably a second cousin of William Ball (Harriet and William had had grandmothers who'd been sisters), which would make her eighteen when she surrendered a lock of brown curls. Little detail about her life has survived, which leaves Harriet with a generic biography.

In her social position, eighteen-year-old Harriet would have been consumed with finding a husband. Her parents,

Ann Ball Scott and John Mazyck Waring, wouldn't have let her do this alone, but would have scanned and rescanned the names of the sons of their small social circle. Harriet would have been allowed to attend—and if she disliked the flirting carousel, she would have been forced to attend—a repetitive schedule of dances and teas. Meanwhile, by most of the people around her, Harriet would have been treated like a thing, her beauty and appeal the subject of gossip. A woman in Harriet's situation was expected to be married by twenty-two or twenty-three. A pity there is no evidence of her personality or her desires. A pity, too, that tests on her hair, done by the lab of Dr. Bert Ely, at the University of South Carolina, produced no DNA.

The second stray sample belonged to another teenager. "Adelaide Shoolbred, 13 years, Jan 1849" is a walk-through in the hair collection, a girl connected to the rest by marriage and the only one who wasn't a cousin of some strain. Adelaide had probably left her hair at Limerick plantation during a visit with her parents.

In 1842, Adelaide's brother, John Shoolbred, had married nineteen-year-old Jane Ball, sister of William. This Jane, Adelaide's sister-in-law, may have been the person closest to her, though not too close, since when Adelaide turned thirteen, Jane was twenty-six. I had no trace of Adelaide's later life, but a few details about Jane Ball throw some light on the girl's youth.

Both Jane Ball and Adelaide Shoolbred came from families in which fathers died young. Jane's father, Isaac, had died when she was two, and her mother and uncles and aunts raised her. At nineteen, Jane married a heavyset twenty-two-

year-old named John Shoolbred, from a prosperous family a few miles away. John must have seemed right, reliable, and modest, the rare thing being that he was overweight. His belly was no obstacle to fatherhood, apparently, and Jane Ball got pregnant immediately upon her wedding in 1842. In fact, she seems to have conceived the first time she had sex: Jane's son, John Shoolbred Jr., was born nine months and three days after the wedding. (The marriage had taken place January 27, 1842, and John Jr. appeared October 31.)

For a short time, while she was pregnant, Jane and her new husband set about arranging their lives. But five months after the wedding, John Shoolbred contracted malaria and died. Photographs of Jane from later years show a pained expression, and one imagines that her experience as a twenty-year-old pregnant widow might have fixed that look on her face. Her features also appear elongated, as though her brow and chin are trying to push each other as far away as possible, the sinking expression of grief.

After her husband's death, Jane moved in with her brother, William, and his family at Limerick. When Adelaide Shoolbred came to the house, John Shoolbred had been dead five years, and Jane's son, John Jr., was five. It's likely that Jane's former parents-in-law, on a visit to their grandson, arrived with young Adelaide in train.

Jane Ball Shoolbred, the widow, lived another sixty-two years and never remarried. She diverted herself with her music, playing the beautiful harp she'd acquired in her youth. The harp appears in a life-size portrait that Jane's brother commissioned, which shows Jane at the strings. (The painting, one imagines, advertised Jane's availability for remarriage, but the subject wears her dour face, and the event never materialized.) The harp was sold when the family needed money, after the Civil War, but one of Jane's possessions survived, to be handed down along with the secretary: her sewing machine, the other diversion after the harp, a foot-pump Singer model with which Jane made clothes during the poorer years.

Jane's sad expression deepened with time (although some of this might be blamed on Victorian photography). She died at eighty-three, in Charleston, in 1905. As for Adelaide Shoolbred, after her visit, she disappears from the available records. All that remains is her strand of hair, which, like Harriet Waring's, contained no DNA.

SCIENCE IS ACCOUNTABLE to replication of results. When two experiments deliver the same outcome, the result acquires the weight of truth. The hair had to go to final hands, and these labs had to corroborate results, or nothing could be concluded about the "Indian" and possibly mulatta connections.

At Harvard University, the day after a blizzard, snowmelt dripped under long light, and slush filled the lanes around Cambridge. Tom Gilbert, an ancient DNA geneticist, had come to Massachusetts from Denmark for an archaeology meeting. I planned to give him three of the samples, one of which had never been tested, that of John Ball, the meek, would-be minister. His hair, from a nearly bald head, had been the spindly bunch.

On paper, Tom Gilbert is British, but his mobile life belies it. He'd recently moved to Copenhagen after two years in Arizona. Prior to that, he'd gotten a PhD in molecular biology from Oxford. The son of a British Council worker, he'd grown up in Nigeria, Sri Lanka, Indonesia, Germany, and Spain. He was twenty-eight.

This geneticist possessed hurtling speech, an electric patter that rarely stopped. His personal style was student bohemian: vertical hair, rectangular glasses, pullover with zipper, chunky wristwatch, Afghan mountain hat. Middle height, about 150 pounds.

Tom Gilbert's line of work, genetic archaeology, involved digging up genes, including some from hair. He had sequenced the hair of the "Ice Maiden," one of three mummified children exhumed in 1995 from a frozen mountaintop in Peru; they'd been sacrificed in an Inca rite around 1500. (Somebody had given the fourteen-year-old girl the Ice Maiden label to help publicity.) Gilbert did DNA analysis of the children's hair, in which, he says, "the basic question was, are they related?" Results said the Incan mummies were not related, which led to speculation about how and why they'd died. Gilbert thought three different families had willingly surrendered their children to the state religion.

I'd been frustrated that only a few of the hair samples had yielded DNA, but Gilbert said this was typical. "Some hair has a lot of DNA, some has none," he says. "I've done hair from an Inuit site, from a place called Qilakitsoq, in Greenland—great, very well preserved, with DNA. Also, we got DNA from some hair taken from mummified bison in Alaska, over sixty-five thousand years old. But let's take contemporary pig bristles. I can't get any DNA out of them."

To Gilbert, the hair samples from the old desk were just another archaeology case.

"The art of ancient DNA analysis is to get rid of the contamination and to preserve the 'real' DNA," he says. "This hair of yours is classical in terms of its problems. You have an old sample with very small amounts of DNA. It's probably been handled thoroughly. You have people now who are walking around covered with DNA. They're handling the specimen. Hair is good for decontamination, because you can clean it easily. It's very different with bone and teeth, which are more porous. Bone is like a sponge. You get a femur from an archaeological site, open it, and it's full of mud, because all the earth has been sucked in through its pores. Your sweat, when you touch a bone, gets sucked in, and it's got DNA in it. So you can grind the outside of a bone, and the interior is still full of contamination. Hair, on the other hand is pretty impermeable. So for the DNA on the outside of hair, I wipe it off with bleach. The DNA remains on the inside. That's one kind of contamination, from handling. Then there's background contamination. It's important to test your equipment, doing extractions on nothing, no sample, to make sure no DNA appears out of nowhere—from the air, or from bacteria on the instruments."

Contamination had subverted the first ancient DNA headlines. In the early 1990s, there had been claims about antediluvian genes, Gilbert says, "like one guy who said he'd gotten DNA from fossilized dinosaur bones." No one knew any better, because there was nothing to compare it to. The "dinosaur" DNA turned out to be human contamination.

The contamination game came to an end in 1993, when Tomas Lindahl, a Swedish-born biochemist working in Britain, published a paper in *Nature*, "Instability and decay of the primary structure of DNA." Lindahl said what might have been obvious, that DNA degrades under heat and over time. Which meant old samples made questionable source material.

DNA damage takes different forms, and all of them can botch the analysis. Gilbert says, "What we know anecdotally about damage is that age is bad, water is bad, and heat is bad." Since the hair samples had come from a hot, wet climate, and they'd stewed for close to 200 years, this was bad news for the early results, the ones with "Indian" markers. Gilbert mentions dead-end samples from bogs in Europe. "Bog people" are preserved corpses, some of them thousands of years old, which have been taken by the hundreds out of moors in Ireland, Germany, and Denmark. "The bog people have no DNA in them."

With dim hope of replicating the tests done thus far, I gave Tom Gilbert three of the specimens.

THIS WAS THE corroboration phase, which meant more labs. In its normal operations, the Natural Resources DNA Profiling and Forensic Centre, in Peterborough, Ontario, helps the Royal Canadian Mounted Police to monitor the treatment of wild animals. Canada has less crime than America, which leaves police time for wildlife forensics. The lab in Ontario does genetic enforcement, screening caviar to see that imports don't derive from the endangered beluga sturgeon, or testing the kills of hunters to see whether their game had lived within an off-limits preserve.

Kristyne Wozney, a zoology graduate, would be the analyst to try extraction on the hair. She'd written a thesis on mitochondrial DNA analysis of the Ontario black bear. One of her enforcement cases had involved an importer trying to smuggle banned ivory from Africa. The man had claimed the sculptures he was carrying at the Canadian border were plastic. Customs sent the figures to Peterborough, where

Wozney showed the "plastic" sculptures to contain large amounts of elephant DNA.

I asked Kristyne Wozney to look at five of the hair samples and hoped she wouldn't find beluga genes.

PETER FORSTER, AT the University of Cambridge, has the reputation of a DNA whistle-blower. A 2003 piece in *Nature* reported that on several occasions he'd pointed out mistakes in published mtDNA sequences, which had not endeared him to their authors. Forster believed the problem of data mistakes was big. If geneticists made sequencing errors, their conclusions meant nothing; and if forensic examiners possessed erroneous databases, they made false statements under oath.

Forster works at the McDonald Institute for Archaeological Research, a small contemporary building flanked on four sides by ancient architecture. He's red-haired, late thirties, and fast with his smile. He wears a yellow buttoned-down shirt, olive pants, and gold rectangular watch. From his office, he leads the way down a narrow street, offering a DNA history tour of Cambridge, and in five minutes there is the Cavendish Laboratory, where, in 1953, the double-helix structure of DNA was identified. "So Crick and Watson went to work, just here," Forster says, gesturing. The Cavendish is a plain brick building, four stories, with tall, factory windows. It could be a mill in a New England town. "Their room was on the second floor," he says, "and when they found the DNA structure, Crick and Watson ran out to the nearest pub."

The walk resumes for a hundred yards, to a white stone building with a crowded bar: the Eagle Pub. "Here's where they went to announce their discovery, to a bunch of people drinking beer. They told the crowd at the bar, 'We've found the secret of life!'" It's Friday night, and crowds spill out onto the curb. A blue plaque on the exterior commemorates:

DNA DOUBLE HELIX 1953
'THE SECRET OF LIFE'
FOR DECADES THE EAGLE WAS THE LOCAL PUB FOR SCIENTISTS FROM THE NEARBY CAVENDISH LABORATORY. IT WAS HERE ON FEBRUARY 28TH 1953 THAT FRANCIS CRICK AND JAMES WATSON FIRST ANNOUNCED THEIR DISCOVERY OF HOW DNA CARRIES GENETIC INFORMATION.

Peter Forster browses a screen at his desk. His database of mitochondrial sequences is one of the deepest in genetics, a resource that allows him to run a sequence and return a pretty good haplotype. Forster can say with some assurance that a segment of DNA has roots in the Ural Mountains, the Levant, or the Mongolian steppes. If the two new labs get sequence from the hair, Forster has agreed to scrutinize.

AFRICAN ANCESTRY, a lab in Washington, D.C., would be a third tester to revisit results. The company specializes in sub-Saharan DNA, and the apparently mixed-race Kate Fuller hadn't been typed.

My cousin Catherine Tupper had taken a nuclear DNA test that showed European, American Indian, and sub-Saharan markers. African Ancestry would go at the question from a different angle. As a matrilineal descendant of Kate's, Catherine would share her mitochondrial DNA, so that by sampling a second cheek swab and getting mitochondrial sequence, African Ancestry would be able to look directly at Kate's haplotype, without dilutions.

Rick Kittles, a cancer biologist, is founder of and chief scientist for African Ancestry. He's tall, wears eyeglasses, has a gentle manner, and speaks in precise, complete thoughts. In the 1990s, Kittles had worked at Howard University, in Washington, D.C., where he helped set up the school's genetics program. While there, he'd become interested in remains of slaves excavated from the African Burial Ground, a colonial-era cemetery discovered in 1991 during foundation work for a skyscraper in lower Manhattan.

In 1999, Kittles started compiling DNA profiles of living West Africans, and in several years acquired some twelve thousand Y-chromosome lineages and eleven thousand mitochondrial sequences.

When Kittles was doing research on prostate cancer in Cameroon and Nigeria, he collected profiles, later gathering more in Ghana, Liberia, Senegal, and Benin. "My contacts would bring back DNA samples and share their data," he says. "The way it worked, I would have an agent, so to speak, who would collect DNA samples from people. This contact would first ask a person, 'What are your parents?' People in West Africa use the term 'tribe,' so this was a way of asking, what was that person's self-defined ethnicity? We tried to keep both parents within the same tribe—Yoruba, Mende, Ibo, and so on—for the consistency of the sample. A small portion of the samples come from mixed parentage, two tribes, in which case we do a Y-chromosome sequence, for the father's line, and a mitochondrial DNA for the mother. The cheek swabs would come back from the field, and I would run the DNA."

Within three years, Kittles's database became the largest available resource on sub-Saharan DNA. He realized it possessed commercial value, and African Ancestry came in 2003. The company takes cheek swabs from American customers and runs them to see if they might match an African region or tribe.

African Americans, as a rule, know little about the lives of their enslaved family members, who lived 150 and more years ago. Very few know anything about the initial captives, predecessors who came in chains from West Africa. To address these gaps, Kittles sampled the places where the slave trade had been most intense. In Angola, which had had the most punishing slave traffic to South Carolina, Kittles worked with Portuguese scientists and got access to data on the larger tribes, including the Ovimbundu and the Bakongo. By matching American sequences to similar ones in Africa, Kittles hoped to give people an idea of the ethnicity of at least one of their African predecessors.

As executed by African Ancestry, the DNA screen can have the feeling of a quest: customers seek something similar to the experience that Jews and Italians have when they go to Ellis Island to learn about ancestors who arrived by steamship. Kittles doesn't claim to be able to tell people where their enslaved ancestors came from, which would be impossible. "When you go back three hundred and fifty years, let's say ten generations ago, you have about fourteen thousand ancestors," he says. "You can't tell everything about them. What we can do, with good confidence, is tell you something about your mother's mother's mother's mother, or your father's father's father's father."

One weakness in the promise involves migration and population change. Some tribes no longer live in the areas they occupied during the slave trade, but Kittles says that while internal migrations have changed West Africa, the movement of people hasn't been great. No population change rivals the so-called Bantu expansion, a cultural shift that preceded American slavery and created the modern template of African settlement.

In a few weeks a letter came from Washington: African Ancestry had sequenced the cheek swab from my cousin Catherine. The profile would presumably address the ethnicity of Kate Fuller. Rick Kittles had run the mitochondrial sequence through his West African database, and the software had returned a match.

A "PHANTOM MUTATION," I learned rather late, is a sequencing mistake made by a machine. Sequencing reactions can create a hot area of variation that doesn't reflect a natural mutation. I could find no data on the frequency of phantoms in DNA screens, but the existence of the term was bad news. It happened enough that it was in The Vocabulary.

Tom Gilbert, the geneticist who'd worked on the Ice

Maiden, sent word from his lab in Copenhagen that he'd extracted DNA from three of the hair samples. His email said that no Native American or African markers had appeared in any of them. Gilbert sounded disappointed: I'd led him to believe he might find either, or both.

"William, Isaac, and John Ball," Gilbert emails, have similar mtDNA sequences (containing a T-C transposition at nucleotide position 16,209), which means they probably fall within one common mitochondrial group, which is almost definitely not Native American. Probably not African either."

Gilbert said that he'd done control extractions consisting of an empty tube with no sample, the purpose being to show background DNA, contamination. If extraneous DNA appeared in the lab, it would enter these results. The control had been DNA-free, which meant contamination had not entered the extracts.

The "Indian" results had first come from four-year-old William Ball. They'd been precise, showing mitochondrial variation at nucleotide positions 16,223 and 16,362. Gilbert had not duplicated that result, either in the William Ball sample, or in two others. He said he'd gone outside the hypervariable region to look at other markers, namely, positions 10,400 and 10,873, where variation signals nonwhite haplogroups. (Variation at 10,873 means one is likely to have had Native American ancestry; variation at 10,400, African ancestry.) Neither marker appeared.

Without corroboration, therefore, William Ball no longer looked so "Indian."

"I suspect your samples fall into haplogroup H," Gilbert

emails. Haplogroup H was, for the most part, a population in northern Europe.

THE WILDLIFE forensics lab in Canada had also returned results. Kristyne Wozney, the examiner who'd sequenced contraband ivory sculptures, emails that she'd gotten DNA from the five samples. Because she usually worked on animal DNA, she's worried about contamination, so she'd run the sequence results through a public database, "just to make sure they were human." She'd also tested her own DNA, and that of the other lab techs, to confirm the results weren't from handlers.

Wozney found that three of the five possessed identical mtDNA. "Aunt Betsy, John Ball [the lead-poisoned father, who'd died at twenty-six], and Aunt Cingie all have the same mtDNA haplotype, which differs from the Cambridge Reference Sequence by a single nucleotide, a C at nucleotide position 16,189," she says. The other two hair samples possessed unique sequences. This fit with what I knew from historical documents about the people involved. The three who shared matching haplotypes also shared maternal ancestors. The two other samples had come from people with no matrilineal link. Kristyne Wozney had confirmed the relationships that existed on paper.

PETER FORSTER, the geneticist in Cambridge who'd shown off the Cavendish lab, possessed an mtDNA dataset that contained some twenty thouand sequences from a sweep of populations. I sent one of the John Ball sequences, plus the Isaac Ball sequence, for haplogroup analysis. According to Forster, the sample belonging to John Ball, a son of the allegedly "Indian" Eliza Ball, fit into haplogroup U, one of the main European branches of mtDNA. The database was quite specific. It had matched the John Ball sequence with a contemporary sample from Baile Átha Cliath, in the province of Leinster, Ireland. The result implied some distant cousins of John Ball might have lived in that place.

Pulling out a map, I saw that Baile Átha Cliath (Gaelic: "Town of the Hurdle Ford") is also known as the city of Dublin. Gael-speakers are not typically Native American, which was more evidence against the Indian-family hypothesis. As for the Isaac Ball sequence, Forster said it contained "a curious cytosine insertion" at nucleotide position 16,189. Kristyne Wozney had mentioned the same thing, with a question mark. Forster said this had to be a transcription error by the sequencing machine. In other words, it was a phantom mutation.

Forster had been skeptical of data in the past. In an article in *Annals of Human Genetics*, he'd written, "more than half of the mtDNA sequencing studies ever published contain obvious errors which should have been caught by the authors." The "obvious" mistakes ranged from the description of samples, to misreadings of nucleotides, to a shuffling of the columns in tables containing sequence data. Forster had counted twenty-five papers with erroneous data published in the *American Journal of Human Genetics* between 1981 and 2002, plus others in forensics journals. "Error-free publications on mtDNA sequences are extremely rare," he'd said.

The spurious mutation (np 16,189) had to be disregarded, which meant that Isaac Ball could be placed in haplogroup H, which represented the most common of the white haplogroups in Europe. It was the same conclusion as Tom Gilbert, who'd pointed to haplogroup H for the other hair samples. On a Web site about genetics and ancestry, Forster had this to say about haplogroup H:

> Mitochondrial type H developed in a single female approximately 40,000 years ago in the Middle East, from one of the descendants of the original pioneering out-of-Africa matriline N. Approximately 25,000 years ago, a small number of women with types H and V, and other types, migrated to Europe, and subsequently survived during the Glacial Maximum in Spain or Southern France, c. 20,000 years ago. With the climatic improvement, approximately 15,000 years ago, this group re-colonized the freshly de-glaciated north and west of Europe, and thus became the most frequent Western European matriline, by far. Today, matriline H accounts for c. 60 % of Western Europeans and c. 38 % of all Europeans. Famous individuals with mtDNA type H include Empress Maria Theresa of Austria, whose filial descendants include Marie Antoinette, executed by guillotine in 1793.

With or without guillotine, Forster had contradicted earlier results on every count. Two labs, two failures to replicate outcomes, and new analyses that put the hair sequences in northern Europe.

Until the "Indian" and "African" test results, I'd had no reason to question the family story that we were white to the bone. Then, with an involuntary faith in science, I'd dropped the idea of our whiteness. But with the new, conflicting data, and with reports of sequencing errors, things were ambiguous. The hair collection had lost its Indianness as quickly as it had once acquired it during early research.

MY COUSIN CATHERINE Tupper had agreed to a final test, a mitochondrial screen that would show whether our great-grandmother, Kate Fuller, had carried West Africa markers. Rick Kittles's company, African Ancestry, had run the sample, and the sequence had come back from analysis. "It is with great pleasure that I report our MatriClan™ analysis successfully identified your maternal genetic ancestry," said the report. "The mitochondrial DNA sequence that we determined from your sample shares ancestry with the Serer people in Senegal."

I didn't know of the Serer people, but Senegal had shipped hundreds of thousands of slaves. If Catherine's sequence had roots in Senegal, then Kate Fuller might have been mixed-race.

Senegal, on the coast of northwest Africa, is a former French colony bordered by Mauritania to the north and Guinea-Bissau to the south. It has an eccentric internal border that surrounds the country of Gambia. Both Senegal and Gambia—on maps, the two countries look like one—had contributed to the slave trade.

The Serer tribe is the second-largest ethnic group in Senegal, where it makes up 15 percent of the population. Oral tradition among the Serer states that they first came to central Senegal from the north, about a thousand years ago. They're Muslim, live mainly along the Senegal River, and many fish for their trade. The Wolof, Senegal's largest ethnic group, have historically dominated the Serer.

I called Rick Kittles for his interpretation, and in his precise way, he said things weren't what they seemed.

"The sample belonged to the T lineage, specifically, the T2 haplogroup," Kittles says. "The T lineage is common in, and originated from, Europe. But when we look at parts of Africa, we see it in appreciable frequencies. For some reason, the T haplogroup is very common in the Serer. It might be due to the movement of women from the north, or due to the spread of Islam into Senegal."

In other words, the sample probably had roots in Europe, not Africa. Kittles's hypothesis was that women from elsewhere in Africa, possibly north of the Sahara, had moved into Senegal, bringing the T2 haplogroup. During waves of Muslim evangelism and conquest, Islam had caused lineages to spread from eastern and northern Africa into the western region of the continent. Some lineages, including T2, weren't indigenous to West Africa, but probably arrived with this migration and empire-building.

"So T, in reality, is a definite European lineage, but it's

also common in the Serer," Kittles repeats. "It's not an African lineage. We see some other lineages, in North Africa, and we know how they came in from Europe. The U haplogroup, for instance, which is European, but is almost always found among nomadic Berbers."

Ambiguity seemed to be the rule. The mtDNA sequence probably originated in Europe, but it also occurred in West Africa.

Kittles says the Senegalese portion of his database had come from two sources. A group from Oxford had done a genetic survey in the 1980s and had shared their data, and a collaborator at the University of Dakar, in Senegal, had provided Kittles with samples from the three major tribes, the Wolof, the Mandinka, and the Serer.

"How the T2 sequence came to South Carolina, we don't know," Kittles goes on. "It could have come through Senegal, or it could have come through Europe. There is still some level of uncertainty. In Europe, T2 ranges from Ireland down to southern Spain. It's one of the common lineages."

More reversed data and another anticlimax. Kate Fuller's genes had probably come from Western Europe, thousands of years ago. She'd been white.

When Catherine heard about the mistakes, the ambiguity and false readings, she was frustrated. "The results had made me change my perception of myself," she says. "I'd been thinking, I'm Native American and part African American. Is that now refuted?"

It had become very doubtful.

"They're saying all over the place that DNA is infallible,"

Catherine says. "There's been a lot of radioactive family fallout from this, these tests. What's shocking is that they're sending people to death and to prison based on DNA evidence."

DNA, the sacred substance with its mystical aura. A crack opened in the religion of science.

13 *Deep Time*

I'D BEEN SKEPTICAL of the swagger of science before entering its molecular world, and now DNA wasn't the field of truths it claimed to be. The outcome reminded me, somewhat unexpectedly, of something from childhood.

I remember that he wore a stiff white collar and black clergyman's suit every day, and he smoked non-filter Kool cigarettes. (When Brown & Williamson stopped making them without filters, he was disappointed.) My father was a minister, and he was introverted for a man supposed to run a congregation. (From the wings, a genetic determinist, in a nasal voice: "the gene for detachment?") He killed himself when I was twelve, after five years of serious illness. My mother was also a church person, having worked as a secretary to a bishop before she married my father.

The church was all around, and sometimes we lived next to it. I spent days in my father's churches, straightening the hymnals, looking for him ("Get your father for dinner"), going to choir practice. This was during the week, and the pews in the nave were usually empty. The candlesticks on the altar glittered, and so did the bookstand used for readings, a brass lectern in the shape of an eagle that held a big bible. Dad sometimes used incense during the service, and on Mondays you could smell it in the air, an acrid and fruity scent that had clung to the walls.

For me, that frankincense traces the footprint of science. Reading science stories in the papers ("Dolly, the cloned sheep, took her last breath today . . .") and watching reporters amazed by technology, I think of the church. Having a childhood of processions and hymns, you notice when reverence comes up the aisle. When science appears in the media, the incense starts to smell.

I want to say a few things about science that will sound out of phase, because thus far I've been investigating molecular biology, but also out of fashion, because one isn't accustomed to hearing criticism of what people do in lab coats, and what those coats represent. When I finish I'll end with a story, so that these last pages will have the right amount of pleasure in them. Meantime, the skeptic's view.

Clergymen used to intimidate people, who were frightened by the clergy's secret line to God. I remember walking down the street with my father and watching the expressions of passing strangers. "Father," people would say, and then nod. A woman would blink and murmur, "Reverend." People spoke in a strange voice. Once a man came running from across the road, shouting, "Father, pray for me!" My father stopped, and the man knelt on the sidewalk. My mother, brother, and I watched my father open his bible, put his hand on the man's shoulder, and read a psalm.

Granted, these little dramas took place in devout places in the deep South, and they showed the minister's power in that section, an authority absent elsewhere. But scientists in some ways are much like my father was on those streets. They're modern holy men, and not many of them mind being cast in the role.

The art of reading deoxyribonucleic acid is a beginner's game, and in my view it possesses beginner's odds. It's regrettable that molecular biology can see messages where none are written, as though it's hungry for status and thinks it can deliver a truth quota. By investigating a small corner of the genetics empire, the study of ancestry, I found a crack in the foundation: DNA data can be shallow and strewn with mistakes. Genetics can't support the desires people bring to it, yet the science of genes thinks it's good public relations to portray itself as omniscient. In two years of reading, I never encountered a researcher who acknowledged a mistake.

Gene handlers may not encourage phantom data, but forensic examiners and geneticists promote a culture of exaggeration. The overstatement is conspicuous in forensics, where the discourse pulls toward hyperbole, the billion-to-one probabilities, the nondiscussion of mishandled evidence. Corrupted results seep into the pipeline.

We need to unconsecrate DNA and bring it into the secular, flawed world. One grows tired of experts on the secret of life who promise to name genetic causes for cancer, heart disease, or whatever ailment will trap the richest grants. They condescend to people, even as they collect public research money. I look forward to the time that genes become just another strand of biology, not this generation's magic dust, and DNA is just another compound that can be mishandled.

The behavior of reporters makes clear that science is overly revered. Science coverage, one of the Pollyanna branches of journalism, is the least critical, most press-release-dependent job in media. Reporters on science use the minimum of templates. "Scientists announced the results of a study. . . ." "Researchers say they've discovered the gene for . . ." or "Medical experts have revealed a new procedure they say will help. . . ." Pay attention to the science press, and you might think scientists dwell in monastic compounds from which they emerge to make statements.

The script of scientist-as-monk is only semi-unconscious and can be recognized in the official costume, the white lab coat, which many use to smart effect. Little research requires lab coats, but the uniform means authority, so people wear it when they have to raise money or talk to nonscientists. (One geneticist, after we met, asked if he should put on his lab coat "for the picture.") The lab coat is like the dress of the cleric, a symbol of position.

Science is supposed to be about removing superstition and ignorance, but in the media it resembles a religious sect. A sign of its religiosity is that you can't criticize science, or make jokes about it. To do so is to invite bewilderment, or risk being accused of anti-secular heresy (mindlessness, knowledge envy, fundamentalism). Jokes at the expense of science are unfunny insults to the lab coat. (How many scientists does it take to change a light bulb? Three: one to change it, one to accept the grant money, and one to claim the new light bulb might cure cancer.) The joke withers, because no one wants to mock the researcher. Scientists have melded in the imagination with miracle workers, and they are to be held in awe, not joked about.

Without trying to do so, molecular biology offers several elements of religion. It possesses a strong story of origins (evolution); it deals in a sacred substance (DNA); and it has a touch of the ineffable (the enigmatic "molecule of life"). Genetic discoveries purport to offer redemption (the monthly rhythm of genetic "breakthroughs" with vacant promises of medical application). And hanging in the middle of all this is the DNA molecule, which does a good imitation of the Bible, whose mysteries will be the subject of commentary for a thousand years.

GENETICS IS THE ascendant program in science, for better and worse. With the Human Genome Project, molecular biology knocked physics out of the top spot, which it had occupied during fifty years of Cold War as the field that had produced nuclear weapons. Like physics, molecular biology inspires wonder. Many admire it for unlocking the genome, while simultaneously fearing it as the demon that will one day clone humans. Individual gene workers are not power hungry, any more than computer designers, but they will claim a sizable empire in the next few decades. Genetics has colonized agriculture, medicine, and psychology, and old ways fall to the lure of DNA. An unhappy outcome is that genetic determinism becomes widespread orthodoxy. Determinism sweeps aside behavioral explanation and substitutes molecular causes for human messiness. It trickles down to everyday speech, till it's no longer a joke to say things like, "I can't help it, I have the obesity gene."

Is it unscientific to point out how gene research fits the stock-price needs of the medical supplier paying for it? Do the motives for studies become relevant when the data are announced from the PR offices of pharmaceutical oligarchs? I haven't counted, but I would hazard that one-half of the biomedical research articles flowing into the journal *Science*, or the *New England Journal of Medicine,* or *Nature* are greased by corporate funds. Researchers are said to be neutral, even as they take payola to keep the lights on.

The official discourse of the experiment is empiricism, which purports to erase the author, or render her passive. Data are believed to surface from outcomes and present themselves to observers, who then record them. But the empirical method (I know it's heretical to say) is itself tricked up. Leave aside conspicuous things that spin research, like money, prior commitments, temperament, and institutional inertia. The gap in empiricism is at the center, in the author. Science makes no place, either in observation or results, for fantasy and desire. Reasoned observation is the most rare waking state, and yet it's the only mind that science claims to possess. No hour passes without consciousness being soaked by emotional sprays and streams of desire, shocks of laughter and sympathy; and still the scientific observer is presumed to be transparent and neutral. (Irony and reversal: science can't talk about the way the irrational seizes perception, even when neutrality itself becomes an obsession.)

To be skeptical of science doesn't mean you want Tarot cards in place of flight plans, leeches and not medical care. It may mean you distrust subsidized facts, or it means you dislike the way scientific advances are hawked by father figures on payroll. ("Estrogen replacement? It's for your own good.")

Scientists and journalists take refuge in the "truth will out" position, whose argument can be summarized as follows. Call attention, if you like, to mistakes and contradictions, or the role of grants in outcomes, because in time, gradually, the natural world will reveal itself to research. But money and mistakes and self-importance don't come to a halt merely so that truth can pass through the door.

Philosophically, science claims to be the only discourse of truth. What science does is certainly "true," but scientists have no franchise on truth. They track too closely to reason and to observation, fragments of the self, to deliver more than flakes of truth, part realities. It's a curious fact that no one reads old science, because its truths are obsolete, replaced by self-devouring norms of research. (A geneticist mentioned that he hadn't read *On the Origin of Species,* and "feel no desire to," because it was hard going and got a lot of things wrong.) People often do read old literature, however. Literature is myth, but it's myth no one forces anyone else to believe. Whereas science is the story you must believe, even though it will inevitably change.

The situation of genetics (to get back to our benighted hair samples) may be a bit like that of nuclear power in its early days. During the 1950s, the atom became a vista of science, insinuating and promising. As the nuclear plants went up, the energy industry marketed a program to "harness the atom" that had been loosed from its paddock by Hiroshima. Critics of nuclear power were silenced, and atomic publicists fed platitudes to the press, including promises of "electricity too cheap to meter." Things with the atom haven't really turned out. (Three Mile Island and Chernobyl are the only radiation leaks that one heard about.) The plants may be on the ground, but their publicity strategy has turned to damage control, and to say as little as possible, in order not to fuel anxiety.

With the same excitement of the original nuclear ushers, and cheered by unctuous media, geneticists promise to mend birth defects, switch off Alzheimer's, and grow extra organs. Expectations are high, and many are hypnotized. Like the people who bowed their heads when my father went down the sidewalk.

WHICH ENDS THE complaints in these pages against molecular biology, and makes way for the last story—

The individual scientists I'd met had all been modest and endearing. To sample the lives of DNA workers (rather than just look at their labs), one night I went out with two geneticists, both of whom were finishing their PhDs. It was an unscientific experiment, intended to explore my own biases.

New York City, late winter, sundown. We found a dingy

bar where the decor consisted of scarred wooden tables with dripped candles on them, some in three-foot-tall cone shapes. Throw pillows on the banquette showed stuffing, and the music, synthetic tango, required everyone to yell.

Nelson, twenty-six, had a five-day beard, clothing from thrift stores, and unwashed, uncut hair. Had he wanted to be an art student, he possessed the right shape and accessories (five-foot-nine, 150 pounds, dirty canvas shoulder bag). The artsy impression vanished when he spoke, because Nelson's speech bubbled with The Vocabulary. With a beer still en route, he told stories from a recent archaeological dig where the goal had been to find genetic sequences in remnants of food people had eaten thousands of years ago.

Prisha, the other geneticist, also twenty-six, had cleaner grooming and posthippy style. She wore ear-length hair in a 1970s-revival cut, low-waist jeans and a peasant blouse. Her warm and touchy manner could have been that of a theater major, but talk also gave her away. She'd lately spent a summer in Tanzania, collecting cheek swabs from tribal clans.

Nelson, high-spirited, talked about coprolites. "Amazing resource," he says. "Just dried poop, but when you extract the DNA from a coprolite, you can show what kind of dogs people had with them, I mean, ten thousand years ago. Because the human sample will be lying in the same area as the dog sample. At that time, there was little difference between wolf and dog DNA. Except in the case of the Chihuahua, which turns out to have been one of the earliest breeds."

Prisha nodded her head at the value of coprolites.

"Caves are great resources for coprolites," Nelson goes

on, "because animals and people went in there for thousands of years to use the bathroom, and the caves were cool and dry. The preservation is amazing! There was a famous study of three coprolites from Texas, probably five thousand years old, which showed that at the time people were practically eating rope. You can get the DNA and you can see exactly what they ate. When I give talks, the anthropologists often get excited, because they all have coprolites, and they don't know what to do with them. They ask if they can send them to me."

With Nelson shouting over the tango, I thought about the hair samples, and how it was fortunate the family had collected their children's hair, rather than the kind of material Nelson handled.

Prisha had grown up in Orange County, south of Los Angeles, and she complained about the cold weather in the East. But she sounded impressed with New York, especially since her work hewed to traditional population studies.

"People from all over the world are in this city," she says, "and I'm going to write a grant to study the DNA of immigrants. But I don't want to look like a vampire. Collecting cheek swabs sometimes turns you into that. Then I'll get a place on the beach and write about nucleotides and population variation."

As a population geneticist, Prisha had more jobs to choose from than Nelson, the ancient DNA archaeologist. She said she'd been considering job offers around a complex of genes called CYP450.

"I'm looking at ways to get something in the metabolism of drugs," Prisha says. "You know, CYP450."

"No, you mean it?" says Nelson, incredulous. "CYP450?"

A controversy erupted at the table. CYP450 seemed to symbolize a split in the profession.

"CYP450?" Nelson repeats. "You mean, you're going to work for a *pharmaceutical*?"

Prisha says, defending herself, "It's like you think it's dirty working for a drug company. Not necessarily true. I don't want to just help make drugs for stupid things."

Cytochrome P450 (CYP450) is a collection of enzymes that catalyze reactions involved in drug metabolism. Some ten genes (distributed among chromosomes 7, 10, 15, 19, and 20) code for the CYP450 enzymes. The genes differ between individuals, and also between ethnic groups. According to the National Center for Biotechnology Information, a gene called CYP2D6 (cytochrome P450, family 2, subfamily D, polypeptide 6) scripts an enzyme that metabolizes upward of 20 percent of prescribed drugs. About one-third of East Africans have two copies of the gene, which makes them supersensitive to opiates (codeine and morphine), while about 7 percent of whites have nonfunctioning versions of the gene, which makes them unresponsive to normal doses of the same drugs.

The CYP450 enzymes are a focus of pharmacogenetics, the study of DNA differences that affect drug applications. Because the enzymes attract large drug companies, as well as venture capital that wishes to exploit genetics, the subject of CYP450 symbolizes a cultural divide. To Nelson, it separates the people-who-sell-out (working for drug makers) from the people-who-teach (by telling human stories using DNA).

"Not CYP450," says Nelson, shaking his head. "You just don't know what it's like working for a *corporation.*" He spit the last word.

Nelson got to talking about his dissertation, how it continued to be unwritten. "Scientific writing is so condensed," he says. "I mean, most science dissertations are just a hundred pages long. But I'm such a bad writer, I can't get started. And I can't complain to anybody in the humanities. I have a friend who's a historian, and he says we don't write books in science, we write pamphlets."

Prisha wanted a new subject, and she turned the talk to conference gossip. She'd been to a meeting and was reminded how she found it difficult, as a woman in genetics, because she was much in the minority. At the conference, Prisha was happy to have found a woman giving a talk. "That's one person I would emulate," Prisha says and she named a woman I didn't recognize. "On the podium, she has a way of being personal, and at the same time formal. She sort of flips her hair with her hand and says something private, then she hits you with the numbers."

At the same meeting, Prisha, said she'd been disappointed by what she called "the offensiveness of some older male geneticists." She said that one Nobel laureate, in particular, had been in low form.

"I heard James Watson talk," Prisha says. "I mean, he was offensive."

She meant the James Watson who, with Francis Crick, first described the molecular form of DNA, the double helix, in 1953.

"Anyway, at the talk he sort of rounded up his great

contributions, and then all he talked about was girls and drinking," Prisha says. "Someone would ask him about some DNA paper, and he would say, 'Yes, we worked on that, but the important thing was the girls and the beer.' I was offended. He's like, from another century." She waved her hand in the air. "Francis Crick was the solid one in that pair, Watson and Crick."

By night's end, the experiment had returned encouraging results. Nelson and Prisha were iconoclastic, but full of obscure knowledge, and hungry for their subject. They were people with opinions about the figureheads, and not acolytes. Maybe people who do science don't feel its solemnity; the aura comes from outside, projected onto science. Or, maybe younger researchers, not yet in the pipeline, are impatient with posing and scientific pride.

DRIVING HOME IN Connecticut, I passed through old towns with white churches and village greens, along roads that were in use at the time of the Revolution. Before that, they'd been footpaths between Indian villages and cornfields. DNA gives a glimpse of deep time. It can be mind-altering, like historical consciousness. Genes let you see how we bury under asphalt those who came before us, and lets you imagine how we, in turn, will be buried under someone else's.

It would be reassuring to think our muscular civilization might be permanent, but in a thousand years, the cities may be ruins. Cortes obliterated Tenochtitlan. DNA time, an era here or there, implies there will be other cities. The scenario isn't bizarre: clever maniacs succeed at nuclear sabotage or

chemical war, some books and movies survive, and another society grows in the gaps. Deep time. DNA measures thick history, so thick that the story of an incomparably dense society thins to a wafer. And while interpreting sequences and markers, a paradox glides into view, the nothingness of a single life, as well as its infinity.

Ten thousand years ago, people drifted from hill to forest in packs of fifty, teaching themselves how to grow grasses like wheat and corn, and how to keep animals. The drama is written not only in places like the excavated Turkish ruin of Çatalhöyük, a Neolithic site, but also in the nucleus. "Only" 10,000 years back, some adults acquired the ability to drink cow milk, after a genetic mutation that preserved the function past puberty of LCT, previously a gene restricted to childhood. LCT sits on the lower leg of chromosome 2, where it codes for lactase, the digestive enzyme.

DNA science gives its mighty gifts, like a glimpse of ancient people with their cattle, their changing skin color, and their spurts of lactase. A long molecule like a lever that pries open a vista. Although one would like the picture more with fewer mirages in the foreground.

Acknowledgments

For research assistance, interviews, and lab work, grateful acknowledgment is made to Barbara Bramanti, Greg Brownless, Joachim Burger, Larry Cartmell, Amarjit Chahal, Roxanne Chan, Bert Ely, Henry Erlich, Jason Eshleman, Bob Faires, Peter Forster, David Gelfand, Tom Gilbert, Peter Gill, Bernd Herrmann, Russell Higuchi, Carsten Hohoff, Suzanne Hummel, Alec Jeffreys, Mark Jobling, Roy King, Rick Kittles, Sharon Seidel Lee, Ripan Malhi, Terry Melton, Kary Mullis, Nancy Mullis, Heidi Pfeiffer, Mark Shriver, Frank Stephenson, Bryan Sykes, Peter Underhill, Victor Weedn, Paul Wilson, and Kristyne Wozney. Thanks to the late Jane and Sandy Gilchrist for sharing their hoard of antiques and papers, and to Jack Alterman for photography. I'm grateful to my cousins Jeff Ball and Catherine Tupper for submitting to DNA tests and exploring their implications. My wife, Liz, contributed to this book, giving me time and helping in unnamable ways. Thank you to my agent, Kris Dahl; to editor Geoff Kloske, who accepted the idea for this story when he was at Simon & Schuster; and to Sarah Hochman, who improved and edited the manuscript.

Index

Page numbers in *italics* refer to illustrations.

Index

Index

Photo Credits

Pages 4, 54, 74, 90, 136, 152, 214, 217, and 250: Jack Alterman, Alterman Studios, Charleston, South Carolina, 2003.

Page 12: author, 2002.

Page 33: illustration copyright 2002, Mitomap.org; courtesy of MITOMAP: A Human Mitochondrial Genome Database. http://www.mitomap.org, 2007.

Page 58: "The Seven Sutherland Sisters (and one brother)," ca. 1890; public domain photo courtesy of Alan Parenti, webmaster, Rapunzelsdelight.com, June 17, 2007. http://www.rapunzelsdelight.com/images/sut/suther land_sisters.htm.

Page 106: Katherine Fuller, ca. 1890; courtesy of Catherine Tupper, 2005.

Photo Credits

[illegible]

About the Author

Edward Ball's first book, *Slaves in the Family*, won the National Book Award in 1998. He is also the author of *Peninsula of Lies* and *The Sweet Hell Inside*. He lives with his family in Connecticut.